IMPRINT

Killing Women

**REWRITING
DETECTIVE FICTION**

Edited by
DELYS BIRD

Angus&Robertson
An imprint of HarperCollins*Publishers*

Publication of this title was
assisted by the Australia
Council, the Federal
Government's arts funding
and advisory body.

An Angus & Robertson Publication

Angus&Robertson, an imprint of
HarperCollins*Publishers*
25 Ryde Road, Pymble, Sydney, NSW 2073, Australia
31 View Road, Glenfield, Auckland 10, New Zealand

First published by Angus & Robertson Publishers, Australia, 1993

National Library of Australia
Cataloguing-in-Publication data:
  Killing Women: Australian women's crime fiction.
  ISBN 0 207 17948 4.

  I. Detective and mystery stories, Australian—History and
  criticism. II. Crime in literature. III. Australian fiction—
  Women authors—History and criticism.
  I. Bird, Delys.

A823.0872099287

Cover illustration: Charmaine Brown

Typeset by Midland Typesetters, Maryborough, Victoria
Printed by Griffin Paperbacks, Adelaide

9 8 7 6 5 4 3 2 1
96 95 94 93

Contents

Introduction

DELYS BIRD AND BRENDA WALKER

This book began with the idea of asking writers of Australian women's crime fiction to become the imaginative readers of their own genre; to write about the issues of femininity, criminality and representation which were of significance to them, and to write in a form which was not necessarily constrained by the conventions of critical discourse. This introductory section is intended as a survey to form a context—historical, sociopolitical and theoretical—for those issues as they have been taken up by women writers of crime fiction in Australia.

AUSTRALIA'S HISTORY OF CRIME

Crime has marked European Australian society from its beginnings. Its first settlements were penal colonies made up of soldiers and convicts; embryonic social worlds that were starkly structured by the simple dualism of gaoler and gaoled. Robert Hughes's narrative of these beginnings in *The Fatal Shore* presents the compelling idea of a social world formed by a criminal underclass and their keepers; a world of appalling violence inflicted on the criminal majority, the convicts. Equally appalling, though, was the deprivation suffered by both convicts and masters, all of whom were symbolically and literally imprisoned in their strange new world.

Opinion is divided about the imperialist imperatives of the British government's colonising ambitions for Australia, but what was then and has remained the most significant meaning of that experiment in colonising was its unique, even bizarre nature; its use of an apparently empty island, a *terra nullius*, on the other side of the world as a natural gaol. 'Nothing,' Hughes says in his opening remarks, 'in earlier penology compares with it.'[1] These beginnings have only recently been thoroughly examined and analysed: as a nation and as individuals, white Australians have until now either buried or mythologised that penal past.

Accompanying the knowledge of our criminal beginnings is the crime perpetrated by the colonial government on the Aboriginal inhabitants of the supposedly empty land. This thieving of a land from its people was written, originally, as the inevitable consequence of a meeting between a superior civilisation and a primitive culture. Again only recently acknowledged, these major crimes of illegal land acquisition, cultural exploitation and genocide must now be atoned for. And the dominant structuring of Australian race relations as oppressor and oppressed, which mimics and recalls the simple social structure of the penal colonies of gaoler and gaoled, also has to shift. This patterning and the authoritarian imperialist power, the masculine power, that both erected and justified it underlies and gives meaning to contemporary Australian culture. The act of colonising Australia was criminal, and it was directed through a criminal establishment whose officers were promised land as an enticement and reward for their self-exile. Crime, with its definitive qualities of violence and corruption, guilt and punishment, with its hidden, secretive nature always threatened by ultimate discovery, historically colours and shapes our national consciousness.

This early settlement pattern was also marked by its maleness.

Of the convicts on the First Fleet, 548 were male and 188 female; the gender imbalance remained until after the middle of the nineteenth century. The effects of these unusual aspects of Britain's colonial experiment in Australia on the social structures, the institutions and the myths of Australians are difficult to assess. However, it is clear that colonial Australia understood itself and was portrayed from Britain as barbaric, and that its barbarism was in part explained by the absence of the 'civilising' influence of women, and of female cultural icons, such as organised religion and education. This perhaps meant that the familiar stereotyping of middle-class women in the eighteenth and nineteenth centuries as essentially moral, capable of cultivating and refining their society, was particularly strong in colonial Australia, with far-reaching consequences both for gender relations and for the prescriptions on women's lives. According to these pervasive stereotypes, a gentle woman would certainly not write—and probably should not read—crime fiction. Equally certainly, she would not be implicated in criminal acts, either as perpetrator or victim, and her presence would actually alleviate criminal tendencies.

Writing of the masculine imperatives of a major contemporary mode of crime fiction, the private eye genre, Alison Littler alludes to their connection with the historical circumstances and founding myths of European colonial societies: 'Australian cultural imagery is very receptive to masculinist tales of action and to heroism being equated with violence and male strength because of its strong outback and frontier mythology of the harsh, empty land (*terra nullius*) settled by stoic and brave white men. It is a frontier mythology which is similar in many ways to the white, masculinist, North American version which gave rise to the private eye figure.'[2] While the colonial antecedents of the private eye may be less directly discernible than this suggests, and it may be argued that the differences are greater than the similarities between the Australian and the American versions of the frontier hero, these

3

myths can be seen as informing many of the characteristics of the male hero of crime fictions. Other commentators see the beginnings of this figure in medieval narratives of knightly chivalry and romance.

AUSTRALIAN CRIME WRITING

A history of Australian writing also has its own hidden, only recently discovered, underside. Although crime fiction has been a popular genre among Australian writers and readers until the past decade or so, re-readings through analysis and interpretation and the recovery of lost texts have been rare. Now there are the beginnings of a history of Australian crime writing. In 'The Case of the Missing Genre: In Search of Australian Crime Fiction',[3] Stephen Knight remarks on both the extent and prevalence of Australian crime writing and its invisibility within our literary culture, placing himself in the position of scholar as sleuth in pursuit of this missing genre:

> *Australian culture contains a recurring presence which has melted into invisibility, and that is crime fiction itself. Crime fiction set and produced in Australia is an intriguing subject, but so is the fact that as a genre it has been almost entirely overlooked. The character of that genre and the reasons for its invisibility will take some time and no doubt many investigators to comprehend with any degree of fullness (p. 235).*

Knight likens the relationship between Australian crime fiction and mainstream Australian literature to the essential but habitually overlooked clue needed to solve a mystery: 'One of the recurrent themes of crime fiction is that some things can be so obvious nobody notices them' (p. 235). Once recognised, however, the strength and extent of crime fiction in the field of Australian writing may support the suggestion that there is a contextual influence between the circumstances of the European colonisation of Australia and the subjects as well as the genres chosen by Australian writers and readers. That is, there may arguably be social and symbolic connections between both crime in Australian writing, Australian crime writing, and Australia's recent colonial past. Knight refers not just to the continuous history of crime writing in Australia, but to the prevalence of crime as a topic in Australian literary history. In nineteenth-century writing, he argues, this preoccupation is, like that in Britain at the same time, an 'index to the weight of concern with crime in nineteenth century Australian fiction.' Knight argues that because of the peculiarities of European Australian history 'white Australia was deeply aware of the extent of crime, or perhaps the extent of the successful prosecution for crime' (p. 243). We might wish to suggest that the knowledge of crime is embedded in the unconscious of Australian culture, hence in its literary productions. Knight further contends that Australian crime fiction is much less innately conservative than its contemporary English counterpart, perhaps because of the greater social freedom of the new society; he also identifies specifically Australian crime fiction sub-genres—mining mysteries and black police stories, for instance.

In his brief but intriguing solving of the mystery of the missing genre, Knight uncovers a series of clues. For example, the 'first genuine best seller in crime fiction, perhaps in any fiction' was Fergus W. Hume's *The Mystery of the Hansom Cab*. Knight speculates that it may have been the success of this book, which was 'situated, written and first published in Melbourne in 1886' and which sold perhaps half a million copies in its London edition, that inspired Conan Doyle to begin writing detective stories in 1887 (p. 235). While reading the clues for a reconstructed history of Australian crime fiction is notoriously difficult, given the elusive categories that exist within this broad generic classification, and the way crime writers hide their traces through changing and often elliptical pseudonyms, Knight estimates that the field contains at least 300 writers, 1000 novels and probably more short stories. One of the major trails he traces is marked by gender; many of these writers are women.

However, while the question that prompted this enquiry, 'Why such a vigorous area of literary culture should have remained so little known' (p. 240), is politicised through his argument that publishing practices and the failure of academic and critical attention to the genre in Australia have been major contributing factors in its relative obscurity, Knight avoids identifying sexual politics as part of the reason for the absence of crime fiction from all but the most popular consciousness. Although he claims that three males—Fergus W. Hume, Arthur Upfield and Peter Corris—are the only crime writers most Australians could name, of all the others Knight does identify in this one article as substantial figures in a substantial field at least half are women. And in his long and usefully detailed Introduction to his recent edition of classical Australian crime fiction stories, *Sand on the Gumshoe*, David Latta refers to the constant presence of women in the genre, although he includes in the collection only one woman's story.[4]

Women, then, have always been well represented, although perhaps not so well recognised, among crime writers. The extraordinary story of one of these, a woman whose prolific writing career included her contributing over 'five hundred pioneering stories in the mystery genre to the *Australian Journal*' between 1865 and 1910, has been uncovered by another literary investigator, Lucy Sussex.[5] This writer was Mrs Mary Fortune, who published as Waif Wander and used the initials WW for her crime writing. Sussex discovered the common identity behind these names, and the significance of Mary Fortune to Australian crime writing is now recognised, as is her place in the history of the genre. Characterised by David Latta as 'a Melbourne woman, Mrs Mary Fortune', who 'predates virtually all those woman writers who are considered to have been present at the genre's birth', Mary Fortune is the recovered founding mother of Australian crime fiction. Latta goes on to claim that while 'Mrs Fortune's midwifery is not widely known, Fergus Hume's definitely is' (p. 7). Sussex, meanwhile, is continuing her enquiries. She has discovered that the first issue of the *Australian Journal* (2 September 1865), the earliest and longest running Australian fiction magazine committed to publishing crime fiction, carried the initial instalment of a novel, *Force and Fraud: A Tale of the Bush*, by 'Mrs Arthur Davitt'. Sussex speculates that Ellen Davitt 'may be the first woman to write a murder mystery novel in Australia'.[6] Had Davitt used a detective, she would have been the first woman writing in what was the classic crime fiction mode in the late nineteenth and early twentieth century. Her novel would then have predated the first publications of two American writers; Anna Katherine Green's *The Leavenworth Case* (1878), which is usually cited as the first detective novel written in English, and Seeley Register's *The Dead Letter* (1867), which is now understood as supplanting Green's as the first detective fiction by a woman. There is a possibility though, according to Sussex, that Mary Fortune may be another contender for this place (p. 1).

Since these early writings by Fortune and Davitt, Australian women writers have been active in the genre, just as they have been in England and America. In Australia there have been those like Pat Flower, Margot Neville, Elizabeth Salter, June Wright and so on, whose writing is exclusively crime fiction; others like Miles Franklin and Jessica Anderson who have published one crime novel among their other writing;[7] and some, for example, Elizabeth Jolley and Marion Halligan who will play with the possibilities of crime fiction.[8] And there are many who don't write crime fiction but whose works do contain episodes or elements that draw on, or derive from, its characteristic concerns, in ways that often revise or deconstruct the conventional gender structures of the genre which depend on unequal power relations.

Representations of the structures of masculine power and the criminal abuse of woman are central to Elizabeth Harrower's *The Watchtower*, for instance, and Eleanor Dark's *Waterway*; as they are to Marion Campbell's contemporary novel, *Not Being Miriam*, which is a virtuoso display of stylistic shifts, from densely poetic poetic passages with mythological emphasis to writing where event, dialogue and character are more obvious than style. In detective fiction, style is conventionally subordinate to action, and in this sense *Not Being Miriam* is far from a conventional murder mystery. However a death does occur and a woman is exonerated, if not legally, then from within the ethical framework of the text. No mystery or investigation is required; the text is an exploration of oppressive and intolerable domestic circumstances and the violence these circumstances might ultimately provoke.

CRIME FICTION IN ENGLISH

Edgar Allen Poe (sometimes called the 'Father of Detective Fiction') is considered the first practitioner of crime fiction in English, and the originator of the detective story in its definitive early form.[9] Detective fiction was made hugely popular late in the nineteenth century by Arthur Conan Doyle who created Sherlock Holmes as its archetypal hero figure. Crime fiction was thus established as a genre at a time when increasing literacy, the popularity of lending libraries, and, most significantly, the development of paperback publishing in the 1890s ensured an increasing demand. Then in the 1920s, Agatha Christie perfected the structure Knight calls the 'clue puzzle', intriguing and engaging readers who are involved in solving the mystery along with the detective. Christie has sold more books than any other single English writer. This kind of crime fiction had its peak, its golden age, in the 1920s and 1930s. A generic shift occurred with the beginnings of the hard-boiled American school in the 1920s, establishing the two dominant forms of crime fiction as the classic detective story and the private eye story. After the Second World War the police procedural, very popular in television and radio serials, was another offshoot, as are spy thrillers such as the James Bond series.

In this broad generic category—which encompasses detective fiction, thrillers and murder mysteries—some features are easy to identify. It has a consistent set of conventions which are familiar to the reader; it is about the investigation of intention and action; it is a popular form which draws on popular culture; and it assumes social confidence, if a cynically qualified confidence, in the individual investigator and in principles of justice or at least retribution. Having said this, the distance between the social expectations and literary conventions that govern murder mysteries in the British style and the American detective story is considerable. Each appeals to a different caste and location, and therefore constructs a quite different sense of the possibilities of identity and action. Always popular in Australia, crime fiction is now especially so, perhaps in response to the more public exposure of official corruptibility through Royal Commissions and other sanctioned inquiries into the injustices of institutions, from prisons to political parties; perhaps too in response to an awareness that this is a literary form which offers more humour and flexibility than its initial classification may suggest; also perhaps for additional pragmatic reasons, because genre fiction, particularly crime fiction, always sells well, an important factor in recessionary times when any publication is risky.

The stereotypical view of crime fiction is that it is conservative and moralistic, simplistic in its style and punitive in its values. For people who don't like it, it is simplistic in its values and punitive in its style as well. It lends itself, according to this view, to the worst excesses of violence, bigotry and social conservatism. Of course, this stereotype applies most comfortably to so-called hard-boiled American detective fiction, and it doesn't give a very accurate picture of that. Yet detective fiction, like all crime fiction, does have a confident ethical schema, and one which is particularly significant for women, if we accept Marele Day's proposition that 'the hard-boiled stuff . . . [is] the last bastion of masculinity'.[10] Action and authority in the conventional detective novel belong to men. At one extreme of the genre, women are victimised and alluring: worse, their victimisation is part of their allure. In a selection of Carter Brown titles, death and feminine sexuality are joined in bold declarations which unwittingly and ironically betray a fear of that sexuality. *Murder is My Mistress, Swan Song for a Siren, Miss Called Murder, Kiss and Kill, Kiss Me Deadly*—in these titles sexuality, and in particular, women's sexuality, is overlaid with annihilation.

Both the resurgence of the popularity of crime fiction and the recent critical attention it has attracted invite speculation about the functions of the genre in relation to its historical and social contexts, and its readership. Traditional critical opinion has argued that it functions to displace anxieties about social violence and anarchy, the control of crime and so on. More recently, feminist critics have claimed that it represents another form of patriarchal control over women; and that the conventional portrayal of women as alluring victims reinforces this destructive stereotype. Peter Corris's first novel, *The Dying Trade* (1980), signalled the Australian revival of crime writing, and Corris remains its most popular and best recognised practitioner, with an output which may come to rival Agatha Christie's. At the national level, this revival can be understood as connected with gendered social forces and as taking place, often in its more significant and challenging manifestations, through women's writing in the genre.

Peter Corris is not unaware of the contemporary recognition of the misogynist potential of his form, remarking that 'I do try not to be sexist, not to offend women'.[11] The ideological range of detective fiction, which is by no means exclusively socially conservative, offers him the space to avoid overt sexism. However, what is interesting for the purposes of this discussion is the nature of the form itself, as well as the more obvious narrative politics. Crime fiction invites classification and investigation not from the point of view of a narrow feminist prosecution, in a kind of class action, but rather as part of the forensics of sexuality and narrative structure. An internal interrogation of the form and its potential is already taking place, as women writers, never strangers to crime fiction, are currently using and transforming it for their own purposes.

A series of factors, literary and social, have enabled what might be called the feminisation of crime writing. One of the effects of the feminist politics of the 1960s and 1970s was the growth of feminist theorising, and the contingent and profound impact of feminist theories on literary studies. Women's writing was recuperated and encouraged at the same time as theories of gender in reading and writing were being propounded. So for Rosalind Coward and Linda Semple, women's crime writing has been enabled by, and is closely connected to, contemporary feminist cultural politics: 'the search for a hidden tradition of women crime writers has in part been fuelled by the revival of interest in women writers in general'.[12] Women's presses, too, have foregrounded the difference of women's writing, whether it is perceived as essentially so, a result of discriminatory publishing and critical practices; as a consequence of the way women are socially positioned within dominant patriarchal structures; or as a by-product of reading practices that assumed a naturalised masculine reader.

This self-conscious use of the genre by women writers has given rise to the construction of an alternative history, one that follows the lines made familiar by that earlier, traditional structuring of crime fiction from Poe through Doyle to Christie then to Chandler and so on, but which questions the gender politics that underly it. In 'Tracking Down the Past', Coward and Semple revise this masculinist structure: 'Until very recently,' they begin, 'all the critical writing about Thrillers—an all-purpose generic term which includes mysteries, detective fiction and spy stories—would lead you to believe that the vast majority of important work in the area was produced by men' (p. 39). They point out the unacknowledged irony of this masculine literary history as it traditionally dates the so-called golden age of crime fiction from Agatha Christie's first novel (*The Mysterious Affair at Styles*, 1920) to Dorothy Sayers's last (*Busman's Honeymoon*, 1937), and that includes at least three other major women writers, Josephine Tey, Marjorie Allingham and Ngaio Marsh. Coward and Semple engender the contemporary revival of crime fiction, now often referred to as 'the third wave', which they say 'has received a most extraordinary boost from three women writers—P.D. James, Ruth Rendell and Patricia Highsmith' (pp. 39–40). These women have not only made crime fiction popular again, they argue, they have subverted the traditional distinctions drawn between two kinds of writing; genre fiction (seen as lowbrow and inferior) and serious literature.

Thus part of all this activity has been a re-examination of genre classifications and assumptions, in which 'popular' literature, that 'literary Other' as Wendy Larcombe recently called it, has been recognised as a significant social force.[13] That popular writing is not simply (or at all) an opiate, but represents the tastes and values of many and is capable itself of political activity, means it can no longer be regarded as always innocently and conventionally reproducing dominant mass-consumer-directed ideologies. Women writers of crime fiction, then, working in a male preserve with a genre always considered definitively masculine despite its numerous very well-known female practitioners,[14] might now use the genre in a way that confronted and challenged its maleness. Women readers too could identify with these challenges, or construct their own through re-readings of earlier 'pre-feminist' writers.

There are many recent signs of this new interest in crime writing in Australia, some of which include women and some of which are specifically feminist. Both Collins/Angus&Robertson and Allen & Unwin have a crime fiction list, and these publishing outlets have had a significant effect on the genre in Australia. Wakefield Press is reissuing crime titles in their new Wakefield Crime Classics series. *Mean Streets*, a quarterly journal exclusively devoted to crime writing caters for the new interest; its first issue in October 1990 announced itself as 'timely' (p. 1). The *Australian Book Review* now has a 'Guilt Edge' column for crime fiction reviewing. Philippa Hawker's important *Australian Book Review* article on representations of violence in writing, 'Criminal Intent', discussed the differences she perceives between detective fiction, where death 'is the first part of a process of discovery and resolution and the book always ends with a solution and absolution', and crime fiction, 'which functions . . . to disturb us'.[15] In a series of searching explorations of different texts, Hawker asks what's in it for women readers, since it is so often the case that crime fiction has it in for women. The *Weekend Australian* also has a space for reviewing crime fiction, the 'Crime File' column. Although it is by no means non-sexist—one began with the implicit patronisation of 'Recently I've yawned my way through earnest conversations about how, in crime fiction, women writers avoid depictions of violence while the men go to it like rats at drain-pipes', it does include work by women. Wendy Larcombe's terrific piece 'Designer Cloaks and Daggers' considered the relationship between women writers and crime fiction, asking 'what, if any, is the political impact or significance of these books by women crime writers?' (p. 20). Canberra's Wordfest had women's crime writing as its theme and P.D. James as its special guest in 1990, and a recent program of the *Coming Out Show*, 'Sisters in Crime', focused on contemporary American women crime writers.[16] These are local examples, and probably not the only ones.

WOMEN AND VIOLENCE

The significance of women using a genre apparently so dominated by men at least ideologically, and one definitively concerned with crime which has until recently been the province of men in its institutionalised control and solving, raises important issues. Among these is the central question of the ways gender and violence intersect, and the meanings generated by those intersections. The particular conjunctions of women and violence are now being debated and theorised and acted upon in arenas as diverse as public policy—there is a National Committee on Violence against Women, and government task forces on domestic violence—and women's Reclaim the Night marches. The extent of this debate provokes further questions. Do we live in a culture or at an historical time more liable to and addicted to and inured against violence than at any previous time? Are women the traditional victims of violence and/or what happens to women if they enter into structures of violence, in this case writing about women in crime fiction? Does writing about violence make women complicit with it? Do women who are subjected to violence, who are beaten, raped, killed or who are targets of insidious, hidden, violent behaviours—and contemporary studies tell us that at least one in four women do suffer sexual violence before they are eighteen—ask for it?

The Crime File column already mentioned was headed 'Violence rubs off on women', suggesting both that it may, and that it is inappropriate for women to come into contact with violence. Philippa Hawker's reconsideration of her own and other women's—writers and readers—relationship with violence through reading and viewing crime fictions also picks up this idea. The question of continuities between the social realities concerning women and violence, and the representations of violence and women in crime fiction, is one that preoccupies many of the women writing crime fiction, especially those who use a female investigator. They must consider whether violence does rub off on women, and if so, what the effect may be on both categories, women and violence. Further, the question of whether it is possible to write crime fiction that satisfies the necessities of the genre for suspense and fear, for excitingly cathartic resolutions and so on, yet remains subversive or at least questioning of the genre's typical positioning of women is a necessary preoccupation for feminist crime writers.

In *A Room of One's Own*, Virginia Woolf attempted to recover a history of women's lives through a most reputable source, Trevelyan's *History of England*. Trevelyan's index, she discovered, refers to women only twice; one reference was to wife beating as a right of men in the fifteenth century, the second to the position of women who were assigned to a husband as her lord and master at a period some 200 years later. The reality of the historian's perspective on woman prior to the eighteenth century, Woolf concludes, is that she has no place other than to be 'locked up, beaten and flung about the room'.[17] Another powerful image of the way women have been treated in history is located in the practice of witch burning. Like Woolf, we might reflect on the meanings of these socially sanctioned forms of violence perpetrated on women by both patriarchal institutions and individuals. Constructed as weak and meek, therefore beatable, or sexually threatening, therefore having to be burnt, women's public role seems often to have been to provide a legitimised outlet for male aggression.

The specificities of this violence may have changed, but there is evidence of its continuation. For example, a recurrence of the pornography debate in feminism is located in arguments around male economic and sexual control of women through male ownership and exploitation of women's bodies and of the economic structures through which pornographic material is marketed. Marilyn French's new book, *The War Against Women*, is unambiguous in its title and its narrative of men's violent and continuous aggression towards women, across cultures and over time and in many ways. A protracted public controversy over the release of Bret Easton Ellison's *American Psycho* was raised initially by the female keyboard operators at Simon & Schuster, the firm that was to have been the book's publisher. These women workers refused to continue work on a text which presented continual episodes of horrific mutilation and murder against defenceless people, homeless vagrants and women. Opinion was divided between feminist outcries against the book's dissection, often quite literal, of women, and those engaged in the censorship–anti-censorship debate. For Philippa Hawker the most horrifying aspect of *American Psycho* is that the killer is motiveless. Much contemporary social violence appears to be gratuitous, hence beyond ordinary means of control and punishment and certainly explanation. In this climate, the eroticisation of violence through writing which dwells on every torturous and murderous moment is especially to be feared when the murdered body/ies become the feminine body of the text, and the invitation as well as the temptation is to respond with fascinated horror, partaking in the violent dismemberment of that body.

Mainstream Hollywood films like *The Silence of the Lambs* and *Basic Instinct* are part of this phenomenon, in which violence, always sexualised, is itself thrilling. *Silence of the Lambs* encodes in its title the idea of the lack of power of innocent victims, and has a protagonist much like Ellison's. Hannibal Lecter is a glamourised psychopath, so dangerous he has to be kept forever in an especially constructed cell, absolutely cut off from any direct human contact. No attempt is made to try to explain why Lecter is as he is, nor what motivates Buffalo Bill, the serial killer hunted through the film, whose nature only Lecter can understand. Evil recognises and knows evil, and Jody Foster, playing a specially trained police agent assigned to seek the identity of Buffalo Bill and eradicate him, must do so by coaxing the knowledge from Lecter. The stereotyped confrontations between Lecter and the Foster character enact a perverted seduction and are predicated on gendered absolutes. Foster, frail-looking but trained to be physically and psychically strong to fight evil in the American way is a contemporary Beauty confronting the Beast. Does her purity and goodness penetrate his madness? Does she secretly, sort of, fancy him? Certainly the audience is meant to, and did; Anthony Hopkins, who played the monster, Lecter, became an American cult hero as a result of this film.

Basic Instinct presents the same conjunction of sex and violence in a thriller structure, but its female protagonist, a young, beautiful, wealthy, bisexually active woman is given far more power than Foster. Her lover is brutally and graphically murdered at the climax of intercourse as the film opens. She is also the successful author of one thriller and is writing another. The crimes in her novels are ones in which she has been involved—her parents' and now her lover's deaths—and the mystery of whether this is coincidence or an ultimate act of writerly power, in which the subject of reality is reconstructed in fiction, remains unsolved. Not a successful thriller, *Basic Instinct* presents a woman who seems to control and exploit men sexually and who has access to the imaginative organisation of her experiences and their outcomes through her writing. None of this apparent power is realised except in the most trivial and superficial and ultimately, offensive way; female sexuality is conventionally objectified, and the film is both anti-woman and anti-gay.

These texts, and others like them, do implicate us as viewers and readers and do construct in stereotypical ways the social experiences of women. Violence does rub off on women, but latterly women have taken hold of violence in their fictions and re-examined it, often interrogating its gendered meanings either directly or by implication. Violence is seen as routinely sanctioned for certain men—those involved, formally or informally, in securing law and order. On the other hand, violence is never a conventionally acceptable aspect of women's behaviour; it's both not part of the definition of goodness in women, nor is it available to women within a feminist politics. Much contemporary crime writing by women provides a critique of the naturalised conjunction of male private eye and violence, in which the PI's masculine identity is confirmed in his [sic] use of superior physical strength against his enemies, and proven as he triumphs over them. In an analysis of the issues surrounding the contemporary presence of women—as writers and protagonists—in crime fiction, Alison Littler discusses the juxtaposition of violent behaviour and heroic status in the figure of the private eye to suggest ways of reading women in this role. She quotes Jerry Palmer, who 'argues that violence between the hero and the villain has to be read differently so that readers can stay on the side of the angels'.[18] Palmer says:

> *violence by the hero . . . is intended to* exhilarate *the reader: since we are on his side, and believe that he is justified, we are free to enjoy the sensation of suppressing the obstacles that confront us/him. Descriptions of violence by the villain are intended in a different way: they are clearly supposed to nauseate the reader.*

Thus the depictions of violence, which are a characteristic not of classic detective fiction, where horrible things always happen beyond the margins of the text, but which are integral to hard-boiled fiction, allow readers to participate in it vicariously. The 'superiority of the central heroic figure' is ensured by the 'moral sanction of his fictive world'.[19] The logic of the text establishes a hierarchy of value in which the violence is either condoned or condemned according to who is using it and why. But of course the violence remains, and as Littler argues, the 'important issue is the values which underlie, justify and valorise the behaviour' (p. 131). These are clearly masculinist values, endorsed in and through a male world of crime fiction, in which women are excluded from power and control, and often, or characteristically, made objects of the violence.

GENDER, WRITING AND READING

Writing of the ways crime novels construct desire for the compulsive reader who wants more than anything to discover whodunit, Dennis Porter recalls Roland Barthes's analogous linking of this reader of detective novels to 'a schoolboy at a burlesque show; he is so aroused in his desire to see the female sex organ that he is tempted to rush the stage in order to help the stripper strip faster'.[20] He then gives examples of texts which do not simply move forward to their final revelation, but digress; where the reading pleasure is as much in the digressions, which function both to prolong the narrative suspense and to entertain the reader, as it is in the desire to discover the hidden secret. Porter cites Ian Fleming's recurrent use of women and cars as digressive mechanisms 'for the obvious reason that they are the sexiest machines of the age' (p. 75); these are what Umberto Ecco refers to as Fleming's 'relished inessentials' and are 'calculated to appeal to fantasies of oral, anal and genital eroticism' (p. 77). Porter presents such elements to identify the gender blindness common to criticism and analysis of crime fiction. His central and scholarly work, which establishes a comprehensive theory of crime fiction and a methodology for reading it, nevertheless uses these and other such examples in an unexamined way, constructing an avidly voyeuristic male reader who consumes these pleasurable texts as he [sic] objectifies and dehumanises the women in them.

This constitutes a gendered, readerly and writerly violence against women, or the feminine, yet Porter is not unaware of gender issues. Later, discussing the detective hero, he identifies two distinct types. The 'Great Detective' of the predominantly British (and European) classical or golden age tradition is chivalrous. This is not surprising, he says, 'given the preponderance of women authors [using this form]' (p. 186). On the other hand, the new hard-boiled American detective fiction was defined by its maleness, which was 'not only anti-English and antielitist, it was also antifeminist', and used a private eye who was 'an updated version of a warrior'. This figure depends on a gender order in which the 'equation that equals gentility with femininity, and the civilised life with women's estate, [is a] fact of American cultural life' (p. 184). Porter identifies a 'vernacular style', the 'aggressively male voice' of the American literary tradition, which confirms the equation through a linguistic double standard. Significantly, Porter claims here that there is not only no space for a female voice in the hard-boiled tradition, but that women as agents or purveyors of power have been excluded from it by a gendered caveat:

> *To be hard-boiled and to have retained a heroic integrity was to be a man. The culture had generated no precedent for a tough-talking, worldly-wise woman, capable of defending herself in the roughest company, who also possessed the indispensible heroic qualities of physical attractiveness and virtue. A woman in the private eye's role would [only] have been conceivable as fallen or a comic (p. 183).*

Almost simultaneously with Porter's writing this, Sara Paretsky's V.I. Warshawski in America ended that exclusion, and there had been earlier female PIs of whom Porter seems unaware. Others followed, including less than a decade later Marele Day's Claudia Valentine in Australia. Those women writers using the hard-boiled tradition with female private eyes not only challenge these assumptions but also the social and literary conventions that support them.

Contemporary women crime writers who play with the political possibilities of the genre develop sometimes oppositional, sometimes subversive writing strategies that can both fracture and question its masculine structures and meanings. This may seem to presume that crime fiction is inherently conservative in its literary structures and its politics, and that women will often or always puncture that politics and structure their narratives differently. The lack of persuasiveness of this proposition makes it necessary to differentiate between crime novels written by women and feminist crime novels; that is, between those who are using the genre in order to shift reader's perceptions about its purposes (to titillate and shock in its hard-boiled modes, or to console through the intricate and masterly solving of the mystery in its classical modes), interrogating through those shifts the ways its formulas are gendered, and those who enter into its formulas. According to Anne Cranny-Francis, feminist crime writers politicise the detective fiction genre to 'reveal the practices of race, class, and sexual politics in contemporary society'.[21] She uses works by Amanda Cross, Valerie Miner and Barbara Wilson to illustrate these claims.

In *Sisters in Crime*, Maureen T. Reddy discusses the historically problematical nature of crime fiction for women, and suggests that a 'useful way to counter the marginalisation of women in any genre is to redefine the centre'.[22] This has been going on over the last decade or two, most significantly within women's crime writing. Now critics are reassessing the past, recognising that among women writers of an earlier and even our own age are those whose works, while clearly not consciously using a feminist perspective, deal with issues that directly affect women's lives and that form the content of their novels. Through the formal structures and conventions of those novels, too, they may raise questions that at least interrupt the male arrogance of Holmsean rational thought used by throngs of gentleman investigators; or the commodification of women by the gangs of look-alike, slick James Bond thugs; or the macho toughness and cool of all the hard-boiled heroes who confront the terror of the mean streets which they match, evil threat for moralised but equally violent assault.

Dorothy L. Sayers's *Gaudy Night* is often cited as an example of a work that opens up to question the conventional positioning of women in crime writing; Reddy refers to it as 'the first feminist crime novel' (p. 12). Sayers as a writer usually presented a traditionally conservative value system, which often expressed itself in anti-Semitism and racism. *Gaudy Night* on the other hand explores the dilemma of an intellectual and independent woman, Harriet Vane, who is confronted by expectations that she conform to a domestic role. The mystery at the centre of the novel is not so much that of who is responsible for the acts of mischief in the women's college where it is set, but of how women can live their lives in a male-ordered world.

Agatha Christie, too, is now available to readings that label her work as either conservative or potentially radical. Miss Marple can be seen as the first of 'the traditional do-gooding old maids solving the country house murders',[23] a reading that responds to her as a stereotyped busybody, a feeble female answer to the traditional detective hero. Alternatively, she is figured as a subtle, woman's comment on the meanings of that hero figure, and his use of the twin male tools of reason and science to unravel those intricate puzzles which are beyond ordinary human comprehension. In such a reading, Miss Marples are familiar, not distanced, figures, using their domestic attributes of listening and gossiping, intuition and insight, and a keen-minded, intimate knowledge of their small private worlds combined with a genuine interest in the people in them to sort out the disruptions within those worlds. It is not unusual, too, to find other kinds of woman-centred writing with a female investigator subjected to critical patronage of the sort that labels it of the 'Had I But Known' variety. This not-very-subtle put-down depends on an implicit comparison between the hard-headed, self-congratulatory problem-solving of the god-like hero detective and what looks like a self-deprecatory, more muddled and intuitive amateur female sleuth.

Critical disagreements over whether Agatha Christie can, or should, be regarded as a feminist writer depend, as Marty Knepper acknowledges in 'Agatha Christie—Feminist', in part at least on the critic/reader's conception of feminism. These debates provide a focus for the concerns which circulate through all the discussions around the topic of women and crime fiction, and which underpin even the possibility of such a topic. Knepper establishes her criteria as:

For the purposes of this discussion a feminist writer will be defined as a writer, female or male, who shows, as a norm and not as freaks, women capable of intelligence, moral responsibility, competence, and independent action; who presents women as central characters, as the heroines, not just as 'the other sex' . . . who reveals the economic, social, political and psychological problems women face as part of a patriarchal society; who explores female consciousness and female perceptions of the world; who creates women who have psychological complexity and transcend the sexist stereotypes that are as old as Eve and as limited as the lives of most fictional spinster schoolmarms. In contrast, the anti-feminist writer is a man or a woman who depicts women as naturally inferior to men in areas such as intelligence, morality, assertiveness, and self-control; who dismisses strong women as ridiculous or evil anomalies of nature; who presents only males as heroes and only a male view of the world; who characterises women exclusively in terms of their relationships to men and in narrowly stereotyped ways; who is concerned not so much with 'reality' (women as victims of a sexist society) but with fantasy (men as 'victims' of powerful, predatory women).[24]

This commonsense liberal feminism takes issue with the equally commonsensical but perhaps more radical feminism of two other critics who examine sexual politics in Christie's, Allingham's and Sayers's work. Although their view credits Christie with portraying independent, single women detectives, 'both spinster (Jane Marple) and widow (Ariadne Oliver) are self-sufficient, possessing a zest for life depending in no way on a man's support and approval . . . Christie takes it for granted that without youth, beauty, or a husband a woman can still be fulfilled',[25] they argue that the majority of women in her work and that of the other two writers are sexist stereotypes. These fictional women are shown to be inferior to and dependent on or manipulative of men. When they are shown as strong and independent they are at the same time deadly and destructively dominant, represented in just the way they would be in the most conventional male crime fiction.

While admitting this case, Knepper finds enough evidence in some of the minor novels for Christie's presentation of 'some very admirable female heroes . . . exploring many problems women face as a result of the sexism that pervades our society' (p. 401). In this debate, which depends more on different definitions than on divergent philosophies, both sides rely on lists to support their case (for instance, Knepper lists 'fourteen examples of competent women in Christie's novels', of which 'only three are criminals' (p. 401)). They categorise women, using a notion of a one-to-one relationship between female characters and reality (Knepper refers to Christie's apparent 'knowledge of real women'; 'Only a writer with a healthy respect for women's abilities [and this knowledge] could create the diversity of characters Christie does' (p. 401)), producing 'role model' criticism that depends on the idea of the 'true woman' (who appears in Christie sometimes for Knepper) and the 'false woman' (always in all three writers' work for the other critics).

These assumptions are no longer possible. Not only does the concept of a 'real woman' deny those other categories that intersect with gender, such as class, race, sexuality and colour, homogenising women into one white, middle class, educated mass, it misrepresents the nature of fictional representation, which both positions us as readers and is constructed by way of ideology. It also ignores the formal qualities of the works, including the ways they reproduce generic conventions. The assertion, 'Agatha Christie—Feminist', is thus singular and reductive. Political and theoretical shifts have resulted in a movement away from earlier readings in which feminist critics were 'concerned to show how women's texts were swamped, invaded, imprisoned' by the normalising and normative prescriptions of genre fiction, so that their work reproduced the repressive ideologies that govern any popular form, to a 'concern to show how women as writers or readers can subvert or rework genres either consciously or unconsciously, imagining new possibilities for themselves'.[26]

POPULARITY AND POLITICAL CORRECTNESS

According to Barbara Godard, 'What feminist theory has shown us is that strategies of reading and writing are forms of cultural resistance'.[27] While this may not always be so, it is in the shifts around these possibilities of alignment and resistance to the codes and conventions of crime fiction that our interest in this topic began. Crime fiction is a particularly attractive category to women writers, perhaps precisely because it is so popular. As a popular genre, necessarily governed by strict formulae, it offers contemporary female writers (and readers) plenty of scope for a parodic re-working of its conventionally masculinist. For Godard, crime fiction is one of the genres, 'popular and highly coded', which 'free writers—and readers—from the constraints of realism, free them to hypothesise alternative realities which implicitly or explicitly criticise their own and which locate sexist ideologies and sexist practices as structural determinants of their own society' (p. 46). Although crime fiction, especially in its hard-boiled variety, appears to reproduce a gritty reality, the point is that its quite rigid codes actually allow its users to break free of 'the constraints of realism', opening it up to formal and political (in this case feminist) interventions. The work of Jan McKemmish and Finola Moorhead takes full advantage of those possibilities.

This conceptualisation links to two related issues which are often invoked in discussions of women and crime fiction. The first is that forms of popular culture are not simply repressive, functioning to keep different groups under control through their palatable reinforcement of dominant ideologies, but are 'site[s] of struggle' through which those ideologies may be contested. Crime fiction can be used, then, to express a notion of women's needs. It may 'combat oppression', expressing 'a commitment to political change, and the language of desire'.[28] The issue of desire is the second, located in the undeniable, often irresistible pleasure that comes from this kind of reading. The view of crime and morality and gender relations any text offers may be solidly and conventionally patriarchal. Yet its mystery plot seduces its women readers, who may read from an ambiguous or conflicted position—in thrall to the formula yet resisting its masculine ideologies. The pleasure of the text for these readers is thus quite complicated, including elements perhaps of fantasy and play.

In Britain, and using the classic detective novel as her form, the new Queen of Crime, P.D. James, is one of the writers who has shifted and broadened the parameters of crime fiction. Her books deny the morally simplistic structures and meanings of much detective fiction, presenting an ambiguous moral universe. And they deal with things that affect women's lives: motherhood and abortion, incest and education, employment and the problems of a welfare state bureaucracy; reproductive rights, issues to do with living as a single woman, and women's emotional and economic vulnerability. *An Unsuitable Job for a Woman* announces ironically in its title one area of prescription that limits women's life choices. Certain kinds of work, and specifically the law-keeping professions, are 'unsuitable' for women. Cordelia Gray is young and inexperienced and becomes an investigator by accident when her friend Bernie Pryde, who owns the sadly unproductive and unprofitable detective agency she joined as a typist, dies, leaving Cordelia the the agency. Bernie, who learnt his craft from working with Chief Superintendent Adam Dalgleish, the literate, sensitive detective hero of many of James's novels, has taught her what he knows. Cordelia is self-consciously aware of the gendered anomalies of her position, yet she is determined to remain and succeed in this unsuitable job. She does so more because of her own sympathetic and intelligent working out of the case she is hired to investigate and a strong personal ethical sense than through any learnt skills of detection. A long and interesting discussion of the ways Cordelia is presented as a female detective, and the differences between this presentation and that of James's male model, Adam Dalgleish, concludes that there is a 'sharp contrast' between the two, implied in *An Unsuitable Job for a Woman* by a 'double-voiced discourse between the detective novel as it ordinarily is and the cases of Cordelia Gray which only borrow elements of that format for their central tale but not the full narrative'.[29]

A traditional Christian moral system and a belief in the importance and the supremacy of the law are central to James's novels. Her writing is, she has said, an exploration of 'the bridges of law and order over a great chaos of both personal and psychological [and social?] disorder.'[30] Much of the power of James's narratives comes from the juxtaposition of a system of order and control with that chaos which it is always threatened by and aware of, and which cannot punish the cupidity and venality and corruption, or alleviate the human suffering, that are part of the chaos. James holds up for examination what much detective fiction avoids confronting or even alluding to—the strong sense that while the narrative puzzle, the crime, may be solved, intellectually and elegantly, there is no solution to the rest of the mess, which remains. At the same time, James's narratives can be punitive to women. In *Devices and Desires* (1989), a young woman is stalked and murdered at its very beginning. This chilling opening is narrated in a way that makes a female reader both male voyeur and judge: the woman has disobeyed her father's instructions to catch the last bus home; a serial killer is abroad; she is apparently his next victim; she is a young, unprotected female on the dark empty road alone at night, yet she should not be there. Are we to conclude that obedient daughters will not be killed?

Patricia Highsmith and Ruth Rendell, who also publishes as Barbara Vine, are part of the new publishing phenomenon of socially aware women writers of crime in Britain. More psychological thrillers than classic detective stories, Highsmith's and Rendell's books present worlds lacking the moral absolutes James offers, ones as complex as hers but more unsettling. These writers, Nicci Gerard argues, both 'mark the movement of the detective novel away from [its] traditional function as palliatives to social anxiety' (p. 126). Often the narrative focus in Rendell's (or Vine's) fiction is through one of the participants in the action, ensuring that there is no authoritative position from which to judge actions and motivations. Highsmith most typically manipulates her groups of sick and sinister and psychopathic characters in a way that is as cold and uncaring as they are. As Christie and Sayers did earlier, these writers draw on what Bronwen Levy calls 'versions of feminism'.[31] Their settings are most often domestic; their groups of characters are extended families or resemble family structures; gender relations and inequities and female sexuality are foremost in the preoccupations that direct their work.

Other more politically radical writers like Valerie Miner and Gillian Slovo, in Britain, and Barbara Wilson, as well as others in America, critique the content and the formal structures as well as the dominant ideologies of crime fiction through their writing. As a strategy—using a masculinist, well-defined, highly conservative popular genre to open it up to question from the inside—this always runs the risk of the radical politics being absorbed by these generic conventions and structures. That is, the books must conform to generic conventions and structures to work; to remain politically active, feminist, those generic conventions and structures must be challenged. That writers of feminist crime fiction walk a women's tightrope, suspended over competing demands and interests, is evident from the quantity of criticism that either applauds their work or berates it for capitulation to the demands of the genre; or worries that political (feminist) correctness produces dull books and poor politics or is of the kind that continues to believe this is no place—that it is indeed an unsuitable job—for a woman.

Philippa Hawker, whose perceptive exploration of many of the issues raised especially for women by violence as a social phenomenon and by the representation of violence within a textual/sexual politics has already been referred to, addresses this problem. She uses as an example Joan Smith, a British journalist and writer whose work of social analysis, *Misogynies*, is as chilling and horrifying and compelling as any crime thriller. It is a collection of essays that detail through a series of examples—ranging from Smith's reading of the investigation and arrest of a contemporary English serial killer, the so-called Yorkshire Ripper, to contemporary rape trials, to the ways romance functions to keep women in their traditional place, to an indictment of the latent sexism of Scott Turow's best-selling novel *Presumed Innocent*—the hatred of women that marks and structures gender relations and meanings throughout the history of Western culture. Joan Smith has also written two crime novels, *A Masculine Ending* and *Why Aren't They Screaming?* She is touted on the cover of *Misogynies*, via the *Daily Mail* and in a way that slyly undercuts her own savage critique of the means by which women are judged guilty simply because they are women then punished for it, 'routinely denigrated, despised, segregated, raped, mutilated and murdered', as 'the hottest young murderous woman on the bookshelves'.[32] Yet Smith fails as a crime fiction writer for Hawker, who describes *A Masculine Ending* thus: 'in which Loretta Lawson, academic, stumbles across the murder of an English academic, a dubious type who has been sucked in by American deconstructionists [and who] blunders across the identity of the killer quite by chance. If this is an alternative to the rationalist, reductive, male-dominated traditional murder mystery, I'd rather go train spotting' (p. 31).

Anne Cranny-Francis takes up these issues in her examination of three related texts by contemporary feminist writers, *Death in a Tenured Position* by Amanda Cross (1981), *Murder in the English Department* by Valeria Miner (1982) and *Murder in the Collective* by Barbara Wilson (1984). Reading with regard to the degree to which these works convey a feminist politics through their overt or covert contestation with the ideologies and the conventions of narrative construction that govern detective fiction, Cranny-Francis concludes that these writers, like others, are using crime fiction 'to debate politically radical issues'. She contends further that 'The most fundamental debate in which all are concerned, however, is that of the ideological status and the implications of the genre itself. Each novel interrogates the conservative function of the detective novel and each responds in a different manner to the seductions of its conventions' (p. 82). In this feminist analysis, though, *Death in a Tenured Position* is found wanting, as it is in other such analyses. Finally, it disallows the internal narrative critique a feminist narrative ideology promises: 'In *Death in a Tenured Position* the solution of the crime is that the death involved is not a crime: it is a suicide. And, as I have shown, that result, while acceptable within the tradition of the detective novel, betrays the political practice of this novel, which ostensibly concerns the definition or delimitation of women by specific gender roles or characteristics' (p. 82).

On the other hand, in a witty and wide-ranging short article, Judith Wilt reads *Death in a Tenured Position* as a kind of feminist fable, the story of the woman who made it as a professor of literature and died because to do so she had believed she did not need and must exclude herself from her own community of women; that she had a place as one of the boys and was a part of the false community of male professors at Harvard. When she discovers she has no place, in that world or any other, she kills herself, making it look like a murder. This woman, 'that ambiguous and important figure, that damaging and damaged figure in the lives of academic women, the *Queen Bee*'[33] has always been 'part of a suicidal academic guard'. Using the language of battle, Wilt reconstructs the Queen Bee's doomed position: 'She had been unconsciously reconnoitering territory in a kind of war she couldn't consciously see or support, the war she pretended we didn't (and don't) need, the one she died in, cut off from both the female support troops and the male supply lines' (p. 51).

Wilt's analysis of *Death in a Tenured Position* establishes lines of influence with two earlier novels, Dorothy Sayers's *Gaudy Night* (1936) and Robert B. Parker's *Looking for Rachel Wallace* (1980), mapping a politics of reading and writing through the intersections of feminism with crime fiction, intersections that depend on and open up around, 'the question we ask as detective story fans [which] inevitably becomes a feminist one—playing the game, we wonder, who kills women, and why' (p. 48). Because crime fiction, more perhaps than any other popular genre, involves its readers—a necessary correlative to reading crime fiction is becoming part of the question and answer game that drives the plot as the puzzle is solved, the mystery unravelled, the perpetrator of the crime revealed and punished and so on—then as readers we are implicated in that question. Depending on our own politics, we will be either comfortably or uncomfortably situated in relation to traditional narratives. In others, where the writer is aware that this is a feminist question, our own prejudices may be exposed as we attempt to answer Wilt's question. Her possible answers include: 'Stupid men kill smart women? Wives kill rivals? Jack the Ripper kills "whores"? Powerful men kill women who threaten their power? Man-identified women kill independent women who threaten their men . . . Feminist women kill comfortable or timid women who are undermining the revolution? Murderers kill not the individual but the class or the idea the victim represents?' (p. 48) Much of the seductive power of a crime novel lies in the challenge to the reader to ask the right questions. The closed constructions common to traditional crime fiction and the masculine ideologists they convey together deny questioning of this kind. If such questions are asked, they imply an unexamined 'yes': women are killed because they step out of line, invite or provoke violence, incite male lust and so on. When these constructions and ideologies are contested by a feminist politics, in writing which challenges their premises, then we as readers are in turn challenged.

Suggestions that this challenge—to the genre, thus to the assumptions and ascriptions to which it refers and which it (usually) reinforces, and consequently to the reader—will be judged more or less ideologically sound and successful seems to beg two questions. One circles around the issue of who's judging; a feminist consciousness is based on a range of possible experiences and philosophies and its political expression may take many forms. The other denies the possibility of a single strategy by which a challenge to the conventions and ideologies of crime fiction may take place. Alison Light argues for both the usefulness and the difficulty of genre studies, in the new sense of its being the study of the popular: 'Genre studies seems to me to be useful precisely as a way of prising free and remapping a multiplicity of cultural forms and images. But genre studies can also be a baggy monster, or a convenient holdall into which we throw a pile of very loosely connected items'.[34] Using the television series *Cagney and Lacey* as her generic example, she suggests that neither the attraction of such texts for women viewers nor their capacity to shift accepted ideas about women is dependent on their limitations; for instance, Cagney and Lacey's position as representatives of law and order, or their very qualified liberation; but on the way the series presents its police-detective heroes and the issues they encounter. Many of those issues are central to feminist agendas, as are the gendered themes of the series—the 'unequal position of women at work, the tension between private lives and public position, the relationship of women to power' (p. 32). For Light, it is actually because neither Cagney nor Lacey, the situations they are placed in, or the meanings the series conveys are singularly 'sound' that such a text is both successful and political: 'I suspect that we need to see that it is precisely the unresolvable and the unmanageable contradictions in these images which makes them appealing in the first place' (p. 33).

As many of these debates within analyses of crime fiction as a genre indicate, it is susceptible to interventions from women writers, ranging from those who are aware of, hence challenge, its maleness (of the variety that asserts that women don't fit easily into trench coats, walk mean streets, or think straight) simply by using it, to those who use it for specifically political purposes and to those political ends (actually getting into the coat and on to the streets). But the structural and ideological demands of the genre itself are inescapable, and its radicalisation difficult. Philippa Hawker's assessment of Joan Smith's *A Masculine Ending*, that it fails as a thriller, is precisely because it is a feminist crime novel. The issue of the potential incompatability of a feminist politics and the quite strict rules of crime fiction has preoccupied many women writers of contemporary crime fictions. Also, it is misleading to infer that only women writers with a particular political perspective can or do shift the conventions of the genre. All genres are continually subject to revision by writers; by publishers who label and categorise books, often placing them in a particular pile if it has sales value, for instance; and by readers. However, it is true that a particularly self-conscious relationship has existed between crime fiction as a genre and those numerous feminist writers who have been using it and very deliberately querying its presumptions and limitations in their writing in recent decades. Yet while they may shift the formulae that structure and produce genre fiction, the capacity to radicalise those formulae will be only to the extent that the genre is both recognis-able and intriguing for readers. Speaking about her work and women's crime writing generally on a recent 'Sisters in Crime' edition of the *Coming Out Show*,[35] Sara Paretsky recalled being part of a women crime writers' panel which was attacked by women in the audience for the way they used their feminist politics in their writing. On that panel, Canadian crime writer Eve Zaremba claimed that it is not possible to have a politically correct private investigator; she talked about the 'PI PI; the politically incorrect private investigator'. Paretsky agreed: 'You can't,' she said, 'make a character toe some ideological line. What you'll have is not fiction but ideology'.

That *Coming Out Show*, made to celebrate the so-called third wave of crime fiction—crime fiction written by women, about women and often concerned with women's issues—asked how women's crime writing challenges or differs from the masculine mainstream. While women can't rewrite the rules completely, radical changes to both the form and the content of crime fictions are being made by writers like Paretsky. V.I. Warshawski, perhaps the best known female PI in crime fiction,[36] was created by Paretsky to confront the specifically masculine and often sexist conventions of the hard-boiled genre. Paretsky says she was interested in and wanted to tackle head-on the way that very American form has traditionally represented women. For her, the fantastic capacity of hard-boiled PI heroes like Marlow to live hard, take incredible physical punishment and always triumph is just that—a male fantasy. Warshawski, on the other hand, is fanatical about keeping physically fit and realistic about what she can do, and what her limitations are. Like many other female investigators, she does not really triumph. Paretsky records her own painful consciousness that when she began writing crime fiction, she had to adopt the conventions of the genre, perhaps to compensate for putting a woman where few women had ever been before. She made Warshawski an orphan to reproduce the solitariness of the contemporary PI hero. Then she discovered that she wasn't comfortable writing about a loner, much less a character so absolutely alone as that traditional male PI. For Paretsky, that traditional figure reproduces in the image of the lone individual confronting overwhelming odds who alone is capable of explaining the world satisfactorily a very conservative bourgeois ideology.

This inherent authority and individuality of the classic male detective or the American PI is denied by many women writers. An important part of V.I. Warshawski's life became the people she's close to; those to whom she can turn for help and comfort. This female connectedness cuts across the isolated autonomy of the male PI type. Paretsky sees V.I. Warshawski as representing the enormous changes that have taken place in the lives of women in America in the last twenty years.[37] A woman in a male sphere, her name reproduces an ethnic mix which is very American, and the initials V.I., by which she is most commonly known, give her a somewhat androgynous identity. Only her close woman friend, Lotty Herschel, is allowed to call her Victoria. At the same time, Paretsky says naming her character by her initials was a conscious choice, intended to subvert that male patronage of women, especially of threatening women like the tough and successful Warshawski, which turns their names into diminutives or refers to them by trivialising endearments. To know someone only by her initials may make it difficult to play those male power games.

The key difference between the writing of contemporary feminist crime writers and their male counterparts is the way they represent female sexuality. In hard-boiled crime fiction, a woman who is sexually active is by definition wicked and must be disposed of. This contrasts with a writer like Agatha Christie whose female investigator figures are asexual, none more so than Miss Marple. Paretsky points out that what writers like Christie and Allingham shared with hard-boiled American male writers was that in their fiction virtuous women always have the figures of boys. This desexualisation of early women detectives represents an ideological split between brains and beauty, and relates to the patriarchal stereotyping of women into those who are sexual and wanton deceivers and those who are asexual and moral. As Barbara Lawrence in 'Female Detectives' says: 'trustworthiness could never exist along with beauty and sexual appeal in the same female person'.[38] Bronwen Levy, writing on reading women's crime fiction, identifies the same split around the representation of women in both dominant versions of the crime fiction genre. Women are represented as 'victims or seductresses' in the hard-boiled variety and asexual and outsiders as women investigators in the British school.[39]

Lesbian investigators present an even greater challenge to the macho heterosexuality of both traditional detective fiction and the hard-boiled genres.[40] Kathleen V. Forrest's lesbian Los Angeles policewoman Kate Delafield typifies a radically new approach to detective fiction. For Forrest, the tension between Delafield's sexuality, her personal values, and the hierarchical masculine environment of the LA police force is as much a topic of the novels as are their crime situations. Other writers interviewed in this *Coming Out Show* had similarly self-conscious views about what their major characters might represent, simultaneously speaking differently to women readers and subverting the whole male approach to crime fiction. Kinsey Millhone is the PI hero of Sue Grafton's series of novels which are titled by consecutive letters of the alphabet. Grafton believes women nowadays want to read in their fiction not an escape from themselves but a mirror of themselves. Independent yet still feminine, Millhone for Grafton 'reflects what's happening to women now'. Millhone represents herself as an ordinary person: in the first novel of the series she says that aside from the hazards of her job, her life has always been ordinary, uneventful and good. The protagonist of Barbara Wilson's three crime novels, Pam Nilsen, is an amateur detective and is also represented as an ordinary person. She lives in Seattle, doesn't travel widely and has little experience of the world. Her difference may be seen to lie in her lesbianism and her left-wing politics, but Wilson says she is a very familiar type in Seattle. Nilsen is part of a women's collective and has a twin sister, unlike Millhone, who is by choice unattached, without pets or house plants and on the road a lot. Wilson deliberately made Nilsen an amateur detective so that her experiences with crime would relate to the way crime affects so many women's lives. This exemplifies the double-edged quality of women's crime writing and especially feminist crime fiction. Its politics are auto-referential, subverting in a variety of ways the masculinity of the genre; at the same time the fictions are very closely committed to women's experiences and to issues that affect women's lives, very different in both these respects from the pleasurable masculine power fantasies of male crime fiction.

A range of issues and concerns are central to these American crime fictions. Kathleen V. Forrest writes for a gay and lesbian community, for her the most persecuted minority in the US. She explores issues to do with the level of systematic homophobia that makes gays or lesbians classic victims of crime and of justice. Paretsky is most interested in institutionalised white collar crime because of its capacity to hurt and ruin ordinary individual lives, and because it is so seldom subject to prosecution for that damage. Paretsky argues that although women may be villains in her novels ('I don't think being a woman gives you an arm lock on virtue or morality or ethics') they are not responsible for the crimes, which are always committed by men, and which are produced through the abuse of power available to those men who make up a patriarchal elite, occupying 97 per cent of senior positions in the major American companies.

All these writers emphasise that the primary function of their female investigators is not to solve crime and bring criminals to justice, but to attempt to heal those innocently involved in crimes. This derives from a recognition that both systems of justice and the concept of justice administered through patriarchal institutions and structures is deeply flawed and rarely recuperative for those people caught up in any criminal matter. Paretsky claims that the whole structuring of law and order, of 'making rules and telling people when they've done wrong and punishing them for being wrong', is gendered, 'very masculine, very patriarchal'. For Kathleen V. Forrest, crime fiction can speak to a disempowered gay and lesbian readership, giving that marginalised position a voice and a role model.[41]

The qualified attitude towards justice common to all these fictions is matched by the sense that a central issue is not the 'solving' of the crime but a recognition that crime causes irrevocable change and that the attempt to deal with that effect is at least as important as the larger social outcomes. So Paretsky says V.I. Warshawski serves 'more as a healer than a dispenser of justice', while Kate Delafield for Forrest is 'very vulnerable emotionally, very affected by the grim streets she walks'. Delafield's victories are pyrrhic; she realises that no crime that involves the law can achieve justice in the sense of recovering what has been lost; all she is able to do is to rationalise the events she's involved in through an understanding of them.

Women's crime fiction tells women readers a story about their own lives. It presents the fictional possibility of controlling events and issues that affect our lives and of bringing a measure of understanding to them. The female heroes are strong and capable but not invulnerable nor afraid to admit their limitations or show their emotions, most often sharing an emotional life with other women. They often have the capacity to grow and change within the fiction in a way that denies the static quality of much crime writing, especially in its characterisation. Violence and justice are problematised in these American women's worlds, where the Warshawskis and Delafields and Nilsens and Millhones struggle to deal with them while retaining their own decency and integrity. Differences among women's crime fictions are important and productive; nevertheless, all these writers are revolutionaries, seeking to change the homophobia, the sexism, the perpetuation of stereotypes and validation of violence that are so often part of male crime writing. In this, they activate the potential of forms of popular literature outlined by Jane Tompkins in her *Sensational Designs*. Tompkins's focus is on works which have 'designs upon their audiences', which seek to 'redefine the social order'.[42] In this account of the function and cultural significance of popular genres, their popularity is understood as arising from their ability to 'embrace . . . what is most widely shared' (p. xvi), offering a 'blueprint for survival under a specific set of political, economic, sorial, or religious conditions' (p. xvii). It is clear why crime fiction is again extraordinarily popular in an era when, as we've already discussed, violence is endemic and large-scale institutionalised crime seems to be beyond the capacity of the ordinary individual to comprehend or affect. Such texts, then, may be used to reach as wide an audience as possible, one already established, for political purposes.[43]

These ideas reinforce the significance of the reading process in crime fiction. It is in that process that readers gain an understanding of and a measure of fictional control over aspects of their social world that are beyond their control or comprehension. Each time the formula is repeated, the reader's sense of order is replenished. When the formula is transgressed, pleasure results through recognition of the object and purpose of the parody or critique. In all this, popular literature is much more than simply a form of escape from a less than satisfactory reality, although its capacity for fantasy is a crucial aspect of its appeal. Finola Moorhead recognises this when she begins *Remember the Tarentella* with a scene in a maternity hospital, in which the mother, emotionally estranged from her newborn child, and about to be abandoned by her husband, distracts herself with detective fiction.

As Maureen Reddy suggests, detectives are themselves readers who are presented with a 'fragmented text, one more than ordinarily sensitive to nuances of meaning and its implications . . . the detective must take its signs and turn them into a coherent narrative'.[44] Here again is both the attraction of crime fiction and the central difference feminist crime writers assert over the singular authority of the (male) detective to interpret the fragments of the criminal narrative; to tell finally a singular truth. These writers interrupt this authority, often presenting their women investigators as partial readers, alert to the multiple meanings of their texts and working with conflicting interpretations.

CONTEMPORARY AUSTRALIAN WOMEN'S CRIME WRITING

Crime, as such, is never solved, but justice is brought to bear, or not, on specific instances of crime and this may or may not be intriguing. Literary truths, like the exercise of justice, are provisional and specific to a particular time and place. The contributors to this book are writing at a time when the women's movement has required, though not always won, a more equitable social situation for women; and our systems of justice have shown some responsiveness to this. Feminist theories which speculate about the origin, function and potential of language have fostered and provided a way of reading, innovations in literary techniques and variations from conventionally masculine writing traditions. Contemporary women crime writers, then, have an especially interesting historical position from which to speak about women's involvement in, and resistance to, a literary inheritence which is largely masculine and formally predictable, if not conservative.

Every Australian crime writer replenishes and localises the genre, investing it with a specifically Australian politics and geography. For the Australian reader, there is a double appeal in the use of a familiar form in a familiar setting. Heather Faulkner's Sydney and Kerry Greenwood's Melbourne are characteristic of this. A conscious deployment of feminism, whether it takes the form of Marele Day's inversion of the traditional gender of the detective, or Jan McKemmish's formal dislocations and assignment of covert power to women, marks a further distinctive development of the genre. Australian women crime writers often bring to the genre expertise derived from a different kind of writing: Jean Bedford, author of the Anna Southwood series of thrillers, is a distinguished writer of historical and domestic novels concerning the experiences of women; Jennifer Maiden, whose *Play with Knives* explores the character of a psychopathic killer, is an established poet; Jennifer Rowe, whose insistently Australian thrillers with their deceptively 'ordinary' amateur private investigator, Verity Birdwood, follow the British whodunit model, has worked as a publisher and as an influential popular editor; Finola Moorhead's mystery, *Still Murder*, is an obvious development of her speculative critical work and innovative feminist fiction. Thus national and individual histories and locations are evident in the current variations on crime fiction undertaken by Australian women writers.

Beyond this, generalisation is difficult, given the writers' affiliations with different elements of the crime fiction traditions. There is diversity, too, in the extent to which traditions are followed. In Brenda Walker's first novel, *Crush*, the conventions of detective fiction are contravened or parodied in order to raise questions about justice, authority and sexuality. It is Anna, the writer, not Tom, the lawyer, who finds things out in this novel. Women can unwittingly invite an intimacy from strangers which can be very useful for an investigator and Anna uses this to her advantage.

The paradigm for a masculine higher authority like the law, which is the presiding authority in conventional detective fiction, is of course paternal. Tom is an older, isolated man who had, in his youth, abandoned his pregnant girlfriend. Anna is his abandoned daughter, although Tom doesn't realise this. The characters, then, are always at cross purposes and the criminal investigation happens at the same time as an investigation into inheritance, into sexual and paternal actions and intentions. The authority of the father is linked to legal authority and both are shown to be provisional, questionable. Another significant element of conventional detective fiction which is subverted has to do with observation, with scrutiny. Observation is of course crucial to any investigation. Women are constantly observed and judged on the basis of appearance. Anna appropriates this masculine gaze by slicing out the eyes of a portrait of a misogynist writer and reframing the square of canvas on her wall. She punishes and possesses this masculine gaze, controlling its perimeters (the frame) and its location. Walker says, in short, that she's tried to use and subvert the genre, taking advantage of its parodic possibilities and ethical schema to say something about suspicion, disclosure and authority in terms of men and women.

Perhaps the most controversial works within the genre are those which stretch and test conventions. This category includes Jan McKemmish's *A Gap in the Records*, in which the reader explicitly assumes the role of detective, and Finola Moorhead's *Still Murder*, which is a composite of texts and narrators. Like many writers and critics already referred to, however, Jean Bedford has reservations about formal experimentation in crime fiction, arguing that although 'the detective novel is gaining currency in the presently fashionable post-modernist theory because of its pastiche elements, its irony and its consciously artificial form, as well as its almost universal preoccupation with the underbelly of modern society and the subversion of its icons of power and status', these possibilities should be exploited cautiously, given that 'genre readers do bring a specific set of expectations to the books and their being met is part of the great pleasure of such reading'.[45] In terms of tradition and experimentation with tradition, contemporary Australian women crime writers differ widely in their involvement in, and transformation of, the genre. The contributors to this book represent the range of such diversity.

Susan Geason writes in a clipped, topical, conversationally witty and sensational style, one that follows the American model. In many ways it is reminiscent of Raymond Chandler: the master of laconic humour, action through dialogue and brief sensory descriptions. *Shaved Fish* is a collection of ten polished, balanced crime stories detailing the adventures of a private eye, Syd Fish.

Like her American antecedents, in particular Chandler, Geason has an ear for appropriately bizarre names; names at the very edge of plausibility, which are used not for poetic effect, but as a brief and intense characterisation device. Thus Luther Huck is 'a fat man with a grudge'[46] whose name puts the Mandrake muscleman and Twain's hero in an ironic embrace; Devon Kent is, phonically, a parody of 'heaven sent' with appropriate connotations of the meat market and the (comparatively) affluent south of England; and Grace Ho is a narcotics queen whose trade is neither graceful nor amusing. Not all of Geason's names are as startling and pointed as these. It is a technique which is sparingly effective. However, the active compression of these names is a feature of the narrative style, which maintains momentum by using a kind of tabloid shorthand for city life. For instance, the following description of George Street on a Friday night: 'hoons in V8s screaming tyres and thundering rap music from car radios, crowds of hormone-driven teenagers horsing around, families with whingeing kids streaming in and out of the theatres, buskers murdering a variety of musical instruments, and people clumped around a pavement artist who was reproducing a portion of the Sistine Chapel in chalk' (p. 101) is recognisable, colloquial, but above all, compressed. Street suffering is part of the setting, or the cause of brief indignations. Racial stereotypes—a conventional part of the genre—move the action and humour along. One character is described as 'wearing a Zegna suit and more aftershave than a Mexican airline steward' (p. 5). Syd Fish is against domestic abuse, murder, narcotics, political hypocrisies and an array of general crimes and corruptions which correspond to tabloid ethics.

In *Dogfish*, the novel which follows *Shaved Fish*, similar characterisation and narrative techniques are extended in a story about murder and the development and gentrification of inner city Sydney which invokes the well-known Victoria Street struggle among developers, local residents and Greens in Kings Cross. Syd is cynical and knowing about city politics; he concludes that

'ICAC would be gearing up for a long, hard look at Eastern Sydney Council and Pluto Foods; the shredders would be running late into the night all over the eastern suburbs. And after the publicity died down, the yuppies who bought the Surrey Street townhouses would soon forget the price that had been paid for their dream homes' (p. 190). The city has some surprises for him, including the identity of the transvestite president of the Sex Workers Union, the client who appears in the sensational opening sentence of the novel, whose case Fish finds irresistible. Sexual complexity, in terms of culture and costuming, is part of the plot of *Dogfish*, where gays and transsexuals are presented as both 'exotics' (p. 37) and a hidden part of everybody's background. In Geason's fiction the masculine traditions of hard-boiled detective fiction are absorbed, relocated to Sydney, and put to work, entertainingly and critically.

Women writing in the detective, as opposed to the mystery, tradition, may find themselves in a complex relationship to their predecessors. Marele Day asks whether it is possible to 'put a female in the hardboiled world and have her come across as a female and not as a man dressed up in sheep's clothing'.[47] In the crudest tough-guy school of crime fiction women appear as victimised, manipulative or simply distracting. Working with and against these conventions of feminine characterisation is a considerable challenge for those women writers who seek an alternative to generic stereotyping.

Marele Day uses gender inversions and parody to combat these conventions in her crime fiction. The opening pages of *The Life and Crimes of Harry Lavender* include a scene where the detective turns a blond out of bed. The detective is a woman, Claudia Valentine, and the blond who is dismissed is a man. In Day's fiction, women have authority, including a sexual authority, which is not a traditional part of the genre, where women's sexuality is often seen as dangerous, is circumscribed or regarded as a distraction. In *The Little Sister* Philip Marlowe says 'Sex is a wonderful thing . . . when you don't want to answer questions'.[48] In Day's fiction, specifically sexualised women *ask* the questions.

The Life and Crimes of Harry Lavender establishes the heroine as ordinarily exceptional, with modest university qualifications, a divorce, an abandoned ambition to be a writer, a little karate training and a number of helpful friendships, including a friendship with another kind of investigator, in the police force. Only perhaps in her choice of profession is Claudia Valentine out of the ordinary. It is also a reasonably conventional detective story in which a location—Sydney—is lovingly and specifically described; a network of plausible corruption is traced; and a murder is solved. However, there are comic touches which gesture iconically to the traditions of crime writing, such as the scene in which Claudia interrupts the victim's neighbours as they watch *Murder, She Wrote* on the television; an unusual splicing of the criminal's memoirs, preserved on computer disc, with the account of the investigator; and Claudia, whose investigative skills derive, not from street wisdom but from her university research habits, whose ability to handle herself in a fight is due not to masculine codes of aggression but to women's self-defence strategies, and whose solitude is the legacy of divorce rather than individualism.

Day's second novel, *The Case of the Chinese Boxes*, combines the feminisation of the private eye with a plot which is particularly conscious of women's domestic and commercial authority. Claudia Valentine is hired by Mrs Victoria Chen, a woman with powerful business interests in Chinatown, to recover a key which was stolen from a safety deposit box during a bank robbery. Ultimately, *The Case of the Chinese Boxes* is a story about women: Mrs Chen, her grand-daughter, the child's mother and Claudia Valentine herself. The resources of masculine authority and power—the underworld, the police, the bank robbers, Claudia's boyfriend who can bug telephones—are used by these women for their own purposes. Claudia's boyfriend *feels* used. Claudia concludes that 'All the wheeling and dealing in the city—all the dramas—the biggest ones occurred right here at the centre of things, in the family.'[49] Jean Bedford's woman private eye, Anna Southwood, comes to a similar conclusion about her own successful investigation: 'We'd been so caught up in the public face of things—the conspiracies, the power-mongering, drugs, bent police, the vice and corruption—and none of these was the real story. That had been private, domestic, personal.'[50] These insights are unconventional, in the context of criminal investigation. However, Claudia has been hired because her client thinks that she may turn the disadvantages of her status as a woman to her own advantage. When Claudia is hired, she asks 'What makes you think I can succeed where the police have so far failed?' Mrs Chen says 'You are a woman. You are invisible.'[51] A prevailing ideology of feminine insignificance, then, is useful for the woman private detective.

In *The Case of the Chinese Boxes* Marele Day anticipates and pre-empts the criticism that her character is simply a feminised version of conventionally masculine characteristics by giving Mrs Chen and Claudia explicit insights which would not occur to the conventional masculine detective. But perhaps more importantly, *The Case of the Chinese Boxes* includes a parody of a detective novel which is simply a product of gender reversal and the projection of conventionally masculine desire. When Claudia is in the library doing research on the rituals of the Chinese underworld she comes across a detective novel called *Tong in Cheek*:

> *There was a photo on the cover of a woman in a wig and false eyelashes, baring a breast and a revolver. The blurb said: I'm Cherry Delight and I'm good at what I do. No boast, just fact. With revolver or automatic I can put six out of six in a bullseye, or a body. My hair is naturally red—hence the Cherry—and a Delight is what I am for people I like, or those I want to destroy . . . I love sex and I hate the Mob . . . I can speak six languages and kill without saying a word (p. 123).*

This is a 'bimbo' detective, for whom 'the Tongs were just another version of the Mob'. By contrast, Claudia attempts to understand some of the specific complexities of the Chinese community. Cherry Delight is artificially hyper-feminised 'in a wig and false eyelashes' and her breast and her revolver are given equal exposure. Marele Day has speculated about the woman in hard-boiled detective fiction appearing to be 'a man dressed up in sheep's clothing'. Here she illustrates it.

Femininity, criminality and impersonation are crucial issues in the most recent Claudia Valentine novel, *The Last Tango of Dolores Delgado*, where Claudia, to her surprise, comes to appreciate her transsexual client's carefully fabricated femininity. The plot becomes an investigation into an extravagantly feminine identity, lush, indulgent and irresponsible, a femininity like a 'big Hollywood production'.[52] Claudia's enjoyment of glamour, consumerism and crime itself, in terms of credit card fraud and violence, is unexpected, but as part of the text's larger feminisation of detective fiction it offers insights into women's potential for complicity and complicates the conventionally predictable ethical formula of the genre.

Day's work distances and engages with the largely masculine American PI tradition, feminising it while recognising the fabrications which constitute femininity; domesticating it by merging the politics of the matriarchal family and a more public criminality; complicating its ethical schema by giving Claudia a surprising (to her) taste for consumerism and violence. Marele Day's gender inversion, then, is less of a reversal than an expansion of the genre. How might such expansions proceed? A feminisation of the issues of crime fiction include issues which are specifically crucial to women's survival, such as the issue of domestic violence. This is not unusual in Australian women's crime fiction; Day touches on it in *The Last Tango*; Susan Geason writes about domestic violence in *Shaved Fish*. It provides the motive for murder in Melissa Chan's *Too Rich*. It appears in the work of

Jennifer Rowe and Claire McNab, among others. In *Too Rich*, police detective Inspector Barnaby says 'Not much the CIB or Homicide can do in these cases, except arrest and prosecute.'[53] Such arrests and prosecutions have historically been hampered by a casual attitude to domestic violence. By drawing attention to the criminality and consequences of such crimes, the fiction counters this trivialisation and aligns itself with women's interests. Women's sexuality, too, becomes a possible point of expansion of the genre, as Marele Day demonstrates. Many other writers present lesbian and heterosexually active women investigators. Claire McNab and Kerry Greenwood are notable for their passionate women characters. According to Kerry Greenwood, 'I also had to invent, or discover, a set of ethics for my female hero. Are there different ethics for women? What about sex? What about love?'[54]

Conflict between the ethics of sexuality and conservative professionalism is crucial to Claire McNab's work. Her lesbian investigator, Detective Inspector Carol Ashton, is vulnerable to blackmail attempts because of the secrecy of her private life, while her domestic life is continually at risk because of the distress caused by her refusal to publicly acknowledge her lover. Coming out is not an option for Ashton: 'Announce publicly that you're a lesbian, and to your face people will say how brave you are to stop living a lie and how much they admire you. Then you wave goodbye to your career'.[55] Lesbian sexuality is not sentimentalised: passion is seen as 'sensual combat'[56] and tension and antagonism have a significant part to play in the erotic. Lesbian women, too, are vulnerable to exploitation by straight women indulging a temporary desire for an alternative sexual experience. In McNab's fiction, however, these difficulties are often positively resolved: in *Off Key*, Carol Ashton toughs out a blackmail attempt with the full support of her Commissioner. In *Lessons in Murder* she acts on the attraction which she feels for her chief suspect, thus compromising her investigation. The suspect is not the killer and the attraction is strong enough to sustain an enduring lesbian relationship. McNab's confidence in the liberalism of the police force is perhaps optimistic. Heather Faulkner's *Arlett's Dearth* is much more cynical about the politics of the CIB.

As well as the complexity of lesbian relationships, Claire McNab introduces a number of feminist issues into her crime fiction. The motives for violence against women are discussed. Carol Ashton worries about the extent to which her good looks are responsible for her professional success. She experiences, and overcomes, jealousy of a younger colleague. Different kinds of feminist activism are presented and explored. The showcasing of feminist issues takes place, however, within skilled and formally conventional thrillers.

Conformity to the traditions of crime fiction is controversial. Finola Moorhead argues that 'If one's grand leap into make-believe was role-reversal, or assuming for a woman a job jealously guarded by men, thus accepting reality and showing it as it is, then one is propagating a male view of the world . . .' She also suggests that 'Constant literary experiment is reflective of action in the women's movement, suggesting the question: how can we influence history and culture?'[57] An acceptance and use of formal conventions, however inflected by a view of women's empowerment, may be construed as unacceptably complicit.

Kerry Greenwood uses the traditions of the murder mystery so flawlessly that there is a quality of conscious and comical parody in her work. This parody does not trivialise, rather it affiliates the texts with their feminine forebears, Sayers and Christie. Such pointed affiliation, while not actually experimental, is one way of feminising crime fiction at a formal level. The affiliation is qualified by Greenwood's contemporary feminism, which appreciates the potential for fantasy in this mode and its predilection for ethical ambiguities. As well as the obvious antecedents among women mystery writers, Greenwood's funny and controlled inversions and exaggerations recall G.K. Chesterton, while her social and historical setting give her work a feminine modernist quality, as if her heroine, Phryne Fisher, were the risque cousin of Mrs Dalloway's daughter Elizabeth. Greenwood's mysteries are set in the world of train journeys and picnic baskets, Erté and Chanel, the foxtrot, the Tiger Moth, the Cairo to London Road Race and Dame Nellie Melba. Phryne is the ideal flapper: stylish, sympathetic, pragmatic and rich. She is described as 'being just as truthful as was congruent with sense and convenience'.[58] She has 'no patience with dependence and no understanding of jealousy'.[59] She 'took care of her body, and her virtue took care of itself'.[60] Ethically, emotionally and sexually, Phryne is an independent woman. This is of course made possible by her independent means, the importance of which is never undervalued. Phryne may be an 'Hon.', but until the convenient death of several relatives, she lived in poverty. Her work as an investigator is a serious diversion rather than a necessity. It brings her up against kidnappers, procurers, murderers, rapacious abortionists and other, less spectacular criminals. However, there is subtlety and perceptiveness in her investigations and in the characterisation of her adversaries. At one point she considers Sid, a kidnapper and child molester who will hang for his crimes: 'Phryne wondered how long he had been in love with death. Perhaps the desired culmination of his whole career would be his judicial execution at the hands of stronger men'.[61] This is a significant insight into the workings of authority and sexuality.

The Greenwood mysteries perform a number of difficult manoeuvres effortlessly. They are escapist and pleasurable, yet thoughtful. Luxury and money confer authority, yet this does not seem distastefully materialist, but rather an exaggeration of views such as Virginia Woolf's on the need for women's economic independence in order for them to achieve their full potential. Morality is flexible and Phryne procures for a criminal in order to buy his silence and protect a more sympathetic criminal whom she has released. Yet her motives, which elsewhere are described as 'nothing to boast of',[62] seem acceptable in context. The rigid class structure of the time and place is made to seem innocuous, or else it is inverted, as when a policeman politely fails to correct a tautological classical reference made by a privileged young medical student, although the policeman immediately spots the error, having been well educated outside the public school system. In Phryne Fisher, Kerry Greenwood has created a positive woman investigator who is convincingly ambiguously ethical and who enviably combines pleasure in her investigative work and in her own life with intelligence and useful authority. Too, Greenwood's work displays a feminist awareness in terms of her use of an historical setting in which well-off women were comparatively emancipated; in terms of the treatment of specifically women's issues and in terms of a style which is reminiscent of earlier women writer's achievements within the genre of crime fiction. However, it is not an especially innovative style. Challenges to the very conventions of the genre belong elsewhere.

Jan McKemmish's *A Gap in the Records* works through the conspicuous display of thriller conventions and their feminist appropriation. To suggest, as the blurb of *A Gap in the Records* does, that it 'is a contemporary Australian novel in which a group of women control a world-wide spy ring' is to reveal very little about a text which defines itself as follows: 'In this novel there is no depression, no unemployment, nobody gets retrenched, there are no elections, no coups, no wars. There is no attempt to represent "reality".'[63] This evasive statement is, however, tongue in cheek, because *A Gap in the Records* does in fact document a familiar international political and economic situation where it's all for sale: 'Numbers ideas brains contracts covers telexes receipts dates the time of day' (p. 2). The body, which, in loose obedience to the conventions of the genre, is discovered on page two, is the body of Frank Nugan of the Nugan Hand Bank, whose dealings within the international finance and intelligence communities were investigated and publicised by the *National Times*. Jan McKemmish appropriates him as her victim:

> *Frank Nugan was found dead in his car. The trigger pulled.*
> *The gun goes off. Pop. Heads resound. Panic. Notes are found.*
> *A list of names surfaces briefly, quickly drowns. A most*
> *important scandal this and the telling of it seems to go*
> *backwards, get foggy, muddled as time passes and secrets get*
> *buried meticulously in commissions and reports, bits and pieces*
> *of a marvellous story told by obfuscation, denial and absurdity*
> *(p. 2).*

McKemmish recognises that disclosure is not always informative. In defiance of thriller conventions, the text does not investigate Frank Nugan's mysterious death. The case is not solved, rather, the body is textualised, 'buried meticulously in commissions and reports' (p. 2). Nugan is textually exhumed and briefly examined (as indeed Nugan's actual body was exhumed) in *A Gap in the Records*.

The ultimate display of thriller devices is McKemmish's identification of the reader as detective:

> *To have read this far you have been made*
> *Like a work of fiction*
> *a detective*
> *an historian (p. 111).*

It is often pointed out that the reader of crime fiction functions as a kind of meta-detective, scrutinising the text for clues and solutions in much the same way that a detective investigates material. McKemmish makes this explicit from within the text and the reader becomes the hero, or at least, one of them.

A Gap in the Records does not simply reverse and rework traditional gender roles, offering us a woman investigator in the place of the traditional hero. Instead, a kind of collective heroism operates, where a group of women characters share information and intelligence: 'Power,' as McKemmish points out, 'does not reside in the individual' (p. 93). Her heroine, Mary Stevens, learns this lesson, and the text, with its network of action and influence, its discussion of the global functions of economics and politics, demonstrates this.

Jan McKemmish's second crime fiction, *Only Lawyers Dancing*, is no less skilled; however, it is less formally bold. The point of view shifts to build up a composite of city life, resolving, mainly, in a shift between two women friends: Frances, a photographer and the daughter of a criminal; and Anne, a lawyer and the daughter of a policeman. In this way, the crime fiction convention of a single, central, ultimately knowledgeable protagonist is avoided. The actual crime and adventure in this story seems subordinate to the affections and irritations of the women, the qualities of light and air and city life which they observe and the cinematically sharp diversions into the histories of the characters. At the same time it provides considerable—and chilling—insights into the place of women in organised and corporate crime, as women pay the price—through rape or imprisonment—for crimes which they either did not commit, or did not commit alone.

In *Quilt*, a book of fictions, poems, essays and declarations, Finola Moorhead claims that 'Experimentation with form is an absolute necessity for a woman writer. For what has been done and how that was done neither says what she has to say nor provides the ways of saying it'.[64] It is not surprising, then, that her detective fiction, *Still Murder*, takes such creative issue with the traditions of the form.

Still Murder is centrally concerned with the question of how the heroic identity might be represented. *Still Murder* is a cluster of texts: confession, journalism, computer file, diary, surveillance record and report. Alternative accounts reflect alternative interests. For example, the discovery of a murder victim under freshly planted marijuana seedlings in a public park varies between the informative *Sun-Herald*, with the headline 'Marijuana Discovered in Wiley Park' and the more imaginative 'City Lights Review' which reports the story under the headline 'E.T. in AIDS Scare'.[65] *Still Murder* reworks the conflict over Australia's involvement in Vietnam, and the conflict of the war itself, through contemporary feminist notions of the sexuality of representation. In the process, definitions of madness and sanity, courage, morality and sexual difference are explored.

The focal character, Patricia, is watched. Voyeurism and its motivations is a significant issue in the text. A war hero watches her with desire and she is watched protectively by Margo, a woman detective. Patricia is possibly a madwoman and a lesbian with an oblique view of her culture. For her, heroism is a self-fulfilling narrative, a story which, once told, demands enactment:

> *the woman's story isn't told. The hero comes through it to some fictional satisfaction; the tears and the gnashing of teeth the grinding and damning and swearing at fate itself, as if they hadn't told the story in the first place, planned it all, then lived it (p. 142).*

Heroism is specifically masculine and women are the material for its text: 'Let me tell you there are no forgotten soldiers: the papyrus inscribed with their recall is skin, the skin of their lady-folk' (p. 157). As 'background, location, context' (p. 60) for heroism, women cannot, themselves, be heroic. Margot, the woman detective in *Still Murder*, is explicitly trying to be like a man. Significantly, she considers setting herself up as a gumshoe. However, success in masculine terms involves recognition by men as much as it involves proficiency in a traditionally masculine job, and Margot's boss says: 'Her nose is good but she is not a man . . . She is not a mate' (p. 293). Her situation as a detective is always provisional, supervised by the masculine.

There are both problems and rewards in feminising crime fiction. The appropriation of a form can lead to a regressive reappropriation. It isn't enough to put a breast behind the revolver on the cover of the pulp novel. The gun could backfire. These are the risks of involvement with the genre. However, there are benefits. Raymond Chandler suggested that women write good mysteries because they are (traditionally) patient and observant, without questioning the social structures and ideologies that encourage such 'womanly' virtues.[66] Rosalind Coward and Linda Semple have a tougher argument—they write that 'women's concerns . . . are often the very stuff of the crime novel—violence, sexual violence, conflict between individuals and authority and conflict between men and women'.[67] There is, then, an urgency which goes beyond the topical in women's crime fiction. As well as this, the genre lends itself to inventive transformations from a feminist point of view, because deviation from its relatively predictable form is likely to arouse the reader's curiosity. The stability of the genre makes pointed and instructive variations possible. Ultimately, this formal experimentation and subversion has a great deal to tell us about ideological and literary structures and the interests which they serve.

NOTES

1. Robert Hughes, *The Fatal Shore*, Collins Harvill, London, 1987, p. 2. Not all historians agree with Hughes' depiction of colonial Australia.
2. Alison Littler, 'Marele Day's "Cold, Hard Bitch": The Masculinist Imperatives of the Private Eye Genre', *The Journal of Narrative Technique*, vol. 21, no. 1, 1991, p. 131 (pp. 121–35).
3. Stephen Knight, 'The Case of the Missing Genre', *Southerly*, no. 3, September 1988, pp. 235–49.
4. David Latta (ed.), *Sand on the Gumshoe*, Random House, Melbourne, 1988.
5. Lucy Sussex, 'Cherchez La Femme: Finding Mrs Fortune', *Hecate*, vol. 19, no. 1, 1988, p. 57 (pp. 54–65).
6. Lucy Sussex, 'An Early Australian Mystery Novel: Ellen Davitt and *Force and Fraud*', *Margin* 25, 1991, p. 7.
7. Miles Franklin, *Bring the Monkey*, Endeavour, Sydney, 1933; Jessica Anderson, *The Last Man's Head*, Macmillan, London, 1970. Brenda Walker's first novel, *Crush*, Fremantle Arts Centre Press, Fremantle, 1991, is a postmodern crime fiction.
8. Jolley's story, 'The Widder Tree Shadder Murder' in Stephen Knight (ed.), *Crimes for a Summer Xmas*, Allen & Unwin, Sydney, 1990, is a wonderful parody of crime fiction and of her own style and preoccupations. Halligan, too, has contributed to this collection.
9. Stephen Knight and Dennis Porter both describe antecedents to the formal establishment of the genre which occur in printed and oral texts from the sixteenth century, for instance in street ballads, broadsheets and chapbooks. Both, as others do, identify the Newgate Callender as perhaps its most accessible and usable source (versions of this collection of stories of crime and punishment were brought out from 1773 to the late nineteenth century). Other commentators argue that *Oedipus Rex* was the first crime fiction, and that characteristics we accept as part of the genre today are present in Western literature from that time, while Aristotelian poetics is used in this model to explain its impact, through the traditional devices of suspense, suffering, ellipses and so on.
10. Marele Day, Interview with Stuart Coupe, 'The Life and Crimes of Marele Day', *Mean Streets*, 1, October 1990, p. 57.
11. Peter Corris, Interview with Peter Colton, 'Peter Corris on his craft and Cliff Hardy', *National Graduate*, vol. 2, no. 3, Summer 1991, p. 8.
12. Rosalind Coward and Linda Semple, 'Tracking Down the Past: Women and Detective Fiction', in Helen Carr (ed.), *From My Guy to Sci-Fi: Genre and Women's Writing in the Postmodern World*,

Pandora, London, 1989, p. 40 (pp. 39–57).

13. Wendy Larcombe, 'Designer Cloaks and Daggers: some thoughts on women's crime fiction', *Australian Women's Book Review*, vol. 1, no. 1, September 1989, p. 21 (pp. 20–2).

14. This assumption that crime fiction is a male genre is endemic, and seems to have occurred with little consideration—that is, it's a taken for granted fact, even in studies that consider the ways crime fiction is ideological. For instance, in Dennis Porter's important work, some writers are described as sexist, otherwise gender is not a category of his analysis. Stephen Knight does take gender into account, although it is not a primary consideration in his work; and in other major analytical, historical or theoretical works on crime fiction it is not considered or included.

15. Philippa Hawker, 'Criminal Intent', *Australian Book Review*, no. 132, July 1991, pp. 25–31.

16. *Coming Out Show*, 'Sisters in Crime', Summer Series, no. 1, 27 December 1991.

17. Virginia Woolf, *A Room of One's Own*, Triad/Panther, St Albans, 1977, p. 42–3.

18. Littler, p. 130, quoting Jerry Palmer, *Thrillers: Genesis and Structure of a Popular Genre*, Edward Arnold, London, 1978, p. 20.

19. Littler, p. 130, quoting William Ruehlmann, *Saint with a Gun: The Unlawful American Private Eye*, New York University Press, New York, 1974, p. 3.

20. Dennis Porter, *The Pursuit of Crime: Art and Ideology in Detective Fiction*, Yale University Press, New Haven and London, 1981, p. 53.

21. Anne Cranny-Francis, 'Gender and Genre: Feminist Rewritings of Detective Fiction', *Women's Studies International Forum*, vol. 11, no. 1, 1988, p. 69 (pp. 69–84).

22. Maureen T. Reddy, *Sisters in Crime: Feminism and the Crime Novel*, Continuum, New York, 1988, p. 5.

23. Larcombe, p. 20.

24. Marty S. Knepper, 'Agatha Christie—Feminist', *Armchair Detective: A Quarterly Journal Devoted to the Appreciation of Mystery, Detective, and Suspense Fiction*, vol. 16, no. 4, Winter 1983, p. 399 (pp. 398–406).

25. Margot Peters and Agate Nesaule Krouse, 'Woman and Crime: Sexism in Allingham, Sayers and Christie', *Southwest Review*, Spring 1974, p. 152 (pp. 1149–50).

26. Helen Carr, 'Introduction', in *From My Guy to Sci Fi*, p. 8.

27. Barbara Godard, 'Sleuthing: Feminists Re-writing the Detective Novel', *Signature: Journal of Theory and Canadian Literature*, vol. 1, Summer 1989, p. 45 (pp. 45–70).

28. Carr, p. 10.

29. Kathleen Gregory Klein, *The Woman Detective: Gender and Genre*, University of Illinois Press, Urbana and Chicago, 1988, p. 158.
30. Quoted in Nicci Gerard, *Into the Mainstream*, Pandora, London, 1989, p. 125.
31. Bronwen Levy, 'Introduction to Marele Day: Reading Women's Crime Fiction, Some Problems', *Hecate*, vol. 15, no. 1, p. 44 (pp. 42–5).
32. Joan Smith, *Misogynies*, Faber & Faber, London, 1989, p. xiv.
33. Judith Wilt, 'Feminism Meets the Detective Novel', *Clues: A Journal of Detection*, vol. 3, Fall–Winter 1982, p. 50 (pp. 47–51).
34. Alison Light, 'The Critical Scene', in *From My Guy to Sci Fi*, p. 33.
35. Sisters in Crime is an organisation established in the US by Sara Paretsky in 1986 to make women's crime writing visible and significantly to combat the 'increasing level of graphic sadism directed against women [which is] becoming more and more part of mainstream mysteries'. Of the four women interviewed on the 'Sisters in Crime' *Coming Out Show*, only Sue Grafton is not a member, not wanting to 'toe the party line'.
36. Alison Littler lists earlier examples of female PIs: 'Most fiction using women private eyes as central characters and usually as narrators has been published in the US since the early 1970s. The earliest exceptions to this period, according to Kathleen Gregory Klein, in *The Woman Detective: Gender and Genre*, are Gale Gallagher's *I Found Him Dead* (1948) and *Chord in Crimson* (1949). P.D. James's *An Unsuitable Job for a Woman*, published in London in 1974, predates M.F. Beal's Chicana private eye, Maria Katerina Lorea Guerrara Aleagar ('Kat'), and Marcia Muller's Amer-Indian private eye, Sharon McCone, by three years. Eve Zaremba's private eye from Vancouver, Helen Keremos, appeared in 1978. But it was in the 1980s that a significant increase occurred in women writing series characters in this genre' (p. 123).
37. V.I. Warshawski's appeal is discussed by Linda S. Wells in 'Popular Literature and Postmodernism: Sara Paretsky's Hard-Boiled Feminist': 'Warshawski speaks to the complex needs of the female reader, who witnesses a female detective, competent, autonomous, and rational, but also compassionate, affiliative and intuitive. She allows the reader to experience and enjoy vicariously independence and control when many readers feel themselves to be powerless victims. Warshawski is powerful against the forces of crime. Her power arises from her intellect and knowledge in that she lives by her wits as do all sleuths. She leads an independent life responsible for her own economic and personal welfare. Her romantic life is in her control.' *Proteus: A Journal of Ideas*, vol. 6, no. 1, 1989, p. 54 (pp. 51–6).

38. Barbara Lawrence, 'Female Detectives: The Feminist-Anti-Feminist Debate', *Clues: A Journal of Detection*, vol. 3, Spring–Summer 1982, p. 43 (pp. 38–48).
39. Levy, p. 41.
40. A recent book, *What Lesbians Do for Books: Essays on Lesbian Sensibility in Literature*, (eds.) Elaine Hobby and Chris White, The Woman's Press, London, 1992 includes a chapter on 'The Lesbian Feminist Thriller and Detective Novel' with a long section on Forrest's work.
41. Kate Delafield, as a lesbian homicide detective, can come into a chaotic situation and bring order to it; representing, Grafton says, strength and control to people who have little of either in their own life situations.
42. Jane Tompkins, *Sensational Designs: The Cultural Work of American Fiction 1790–1860*, Oxford University Press, New York, Oxford, 1985, p. xi.
43. These ideas may be linked with those of a range of feminist critics whose work Maureen T. Reddy draws on in a discussion of the appeal for women readers of genres like Gothic and sensation novels, which may be seen as precursors of the modern crime novel: 'If gothic novels are about women's fears and sensation novels about their fantasies, both encode strikingly similar critiques of women's entrapment in domestic life and powerlessness in their primary reality, the family. In gothic novels, the heroine overcomes her victimisation and terrorisation, while sensation novels with female villains offer a transgressive model for women' (p. 8).
44. Reddy, p. 10.
45. Jean Bedford, *Review of Gabrielle Lord's* Salt *and Brenda Walker's* Crush in *Voices*, Spring 1991, p. 100.
46. Susan Geason, *Shaved Fish*, Allen & Unwin, Sydney, 1990, p. 1.
47. 'The Life and Crimes of Marele Day', p. 57.
48. Raymond Chandler, *The Little Sister*, Pan Books, Sydney, 1949, 1979, p. 150.
49. Marele Day, *The Case of the Chinese Boxes*, Allen & Unwin, Sydney, 1990, p. 159.
50. Jean Bedford, *Worse than Death*, Angus & Robertson, Sydney, 1991, p. 156.
51. Day, *The Case of the Chinese Boxes*, p. 4.
52. Marele Day, *The Last Tango of Dolores Delgado*, Allen & Unwin, Sydney, 1992, p. 130.
53. Melissa Chan, *Too Rich*, Spinifex, Melbourne, 1991, p. 42.
54. Kerry Greenwood, this book.
55. Claire McNab, *Off Key*, Allen & Unwin, Sydney, 1992, p. 83.
56. Claire McNab, *Death Down Under*, Allen & Unwin, Sydney, 1992, p. 149.

57. Finola Moorhead, this book.
58. Kerry Greenwood, *Murder on the Ballarat Train*, McPhee Gribble, Ringwood, 1991, p. 15.
59. Kerry Greenwood, *Flying Too High*, McPhee Gribble, Ringwood, 1990, p. 162.
60. Greenwood, *Murder on the Ballarat Train*, p. 61.
61. Greenwood, *Flying Too High*, p. 162.
62. Greenwood, ibid., p. 163.
63. Jan McKemmish, *A Gap in the Records*, Sybylla Press, Melbourne, 1975, p. 111.
64. Finola Moorhead, *Quilt*, Sybylla Press, Melbourne, 1985, p. 128.
65. Finola Moorhead, *Still Murder*, Penguin, Ringwood, 1990, pp. 25–30.
66. Dorothy Gardiner and Kathrine Sorley Walker, *Raymond Chandler Speaking*, Penguin, London, p. 53.
67. Coward and Semple, p. 54.

CLAIRE McNAB

Claire McNab has written comedy plays, textbooks, and for television. She is the author of the fast-paced mysteries Lessons in Murder, Fatal Reunion, Death Down Under, Cop Out *and* Off Key, *all featuring the cool, charismatic Detective Inspector Carol Ashton.*

Killing Women

CLAIRE McNAB

More women now kill. In life, some women take that final, irrevocable step and eliminate another human being, but it is in fiction that growing numbers of female writers execute with words.

And women are captivated by murder as entertainment. A profile of the members of the Mystery Guild, the largest United States book club devoted entirely to crime fiction, publishing around seventy-five titles a year, indicated that the majority of its readers were women who had distinct tastes when it came to mysteries. They said *no* to hard-boiled crime novels, drugs and/or the mob as major elements in a story and to pets being murdered or maimed. They said *yes* to series characters, female detectives, nuns and priests, pets (especially cats) and to whodunit puzzles designed to fool the reader.

The members of the Mystery Guild are only a segment of a huge and varied crime fiction readership. In Australia writers have explored a wide range of sub-genres that draw crime aficionados, but, as in other countries, irrespective of the sub-genre chosen, crime writing emphasises the exploration of character and psychology against a specific social background.

The broad categories are: classic 'Christie' crime puzzle; police procedural; series private investigator, both amateur and professional (including 'I walk the mean streets' tough guy/gal); past era historical; comedy, with subdivisions of farce and 'serious' humour; and political, often feminist. Australia has yet to see the overseas sub-genres of 'cat crime', where felines often solve the cases, or criminal pursuits associated with gourmet food, but we can add our own, possibly unique, category—Dorothy Porter's *The Monkey's Mask* written in the form of poetry.

We may write within categories, but we still have a distinctly Australian voice. Our dry humour and the laconic insouciance that we like to think a national characteristic, imbues our crime writing with a unique flavour. This was an advantage when I offered the first in the Detective Inspector Carol Ashton series, *Lessons in Murder*, to an American publisher. The manuscript was completed in the late 1980s and I decided to try for publication in the United States because the movie *Crocodile Dundee* had created a great interest in everything Australian. It seemed, and was, the perfect time to exploit Australianness as a selling point, a feature I didn't consider at the time to be an asset as far as my own country was concerned. When Allen & Unwin later published the series in Australia I discovered my error. Feedback from Australian readers has consistently mentioned the pleasure of recognising the familiar, as opposed to crime novels set in the United States or Britain. This feedback has led, in later novels, to what might be called writing-schizophrenia, as I've become increasingly conscious of writing for two quite separate audiences—Australian and American. What to a reader in the States is interesting local colour, can be seen here as irritating and unnecessary information. Moreover, although Australian English shows a creative flair that delights outsiders, conversations at booksignings have made it clear that there's always a possibility that colloquialisms in dialogue can lead to amusing assumptions about meaning. In later books I've used Australianisms as a discreet flavouring, rather than an attempt to faithfully record our colloquial speech.

Meeting Americans at booksignings and conferences, it becomes clear that, both as writers and as a race, Australians are regarded as iconoclastic, relaxed, verbally inventive and beguilingly exotic. To overseas readers Australia is a setting still unfamiliar enough to be intriguing. The perception that our mystery writing is different in some way gives us a necessary edge—and such is the avalanche of crime fiction, that any qualities that allow an author or a series character to stand out from the pack can only be advantageous.

In Australia, as elsewhere, crime fiction rides a wave of popularity that has been cresting since the second half of the 1980s. And women are not only writing these novels, they are now creating female protagonists who reflect the great changes our society is undergoing. Why it is that women's crime writing is the genre where exploration of these changes is so concentrated? What is it that a mystery has that attracts and holds such a huge and constant readership, who come to be entertained and are surreptitiously educated in changing social mores as well?

P.D. James has said that we desire the expression of crime, followed by a solution—but not necessarily punishment—as a comforting certitude in an uncertain world. Others have remarked upon the delight of a puzzle, the pitting of the reader's wits against a Christie, Allingham or Marsh in an attempt to solve before the end of the book the who, why and wherefore of a fictional crime.

But perhaps the enduring attraction of the mystery genre is related to our essential natures. All of us contain within ourselves a mystery that might be expressed as: *Who am I, and why do I do the things I do?* And perhaps many, even most, of us have considered murder, however fleetingly. We have exercised our imaginations in plotting exactly how we will dispatch our target. Indeed, if my doctor is correct, competent murderers may be accomplishing perfect murders rather more often than it is comfortable to consider. It is conceivable that some reading these words *have* committed murder successfully. My doctor, a personal friend, mused one day over the cases where she felt a niggling suspicion, not sufficient to refuse a death certificate and thereby initiate a post-mortem and all the attendant unpleasantness, but nevertheless a disquiet that lingered—if an elderly relative who's been complaining of chest pains is found dead, surely it must be a heart attack, not a pillow over the face . . .?

Consider the thought that women write about murder and read about murder because they are more successful in accomplishing this most anti-social of crimes. Not the obvious, brutal murders achieved in the heat of rage with weapons or beatings, but the subtle killings—the poison in a carefully prepared meal, the incorrect dosage of prescribed drugs, the aforesaid pillow over the face, all occurring in the domestic arena where, logically, undetected murders could most easily take place. How many suicides, accidents, fatal cases of gastroenteritis, are to be attributed to the unsuspected wife, sister, daughter, mother, aunt? Not needing to enhance one's ego by demonstrating violence to one's peer group makes for an elusive murderer, whose satisfaction can be discreetly personal.

As women, are we not drawn to explore crime, both in the media and in novels, because we see ourselves reflected there, either as victim or perpetrator? Further, as females we are socialised to learn early that reading motivations is the key to controlling those more powerful than ourselves. It therefore follows that we tend to be interested not only in *who* did it, but *why* it was done. Vicarious victims or murderers all, we are captivated by the deed and all its ramifications—witness the popularity of the darkly psychological studies of Ruth Rendell or her alter ego, Barbara Vine.

Most women are not only physically weaker than most men, they also have less economic, political or practical power and influence. Within the covers of a mystery, particularly of the hard-boiled school, the constant victimisation of women is portrayed with macho enthusiasm. Sex mate, victim, siren, destructive goddess . . . women all share common characteristics—they are inferior to the majority of males, especially the hero, either physically, morally or in the exercise of personal autonomy. And those men they do dominate are wimps, half-men, losers, suckers . . .

In 'real' life, as presented by the media, female murderers receive disproportionate attention. In Australia, for every one woman who murders, there are eight male killers. Moreover, the domestic sphere is overwhelmingly the background for murder, and here up to 80 per cent of victims are women. Yet it is not woman as victim that is emphasised—it is woman as destroyer that galvanises the media. Those few females who kill their partners, often after years of abuse, break the still-potent concept of gender roles. Women nurture, protect, nest. Men possess. And when a male's possession wants to exercise her individuality and leave, she must be disciplined, the ultimate (and often unintended) punishment being death. And the defence? 'I loved her so much I couldn't let her go.'

In the media in general, women who kill are given such prominence that it seems that a female murderer excites twice as much human interest as her male counterpart. This must be so, else why the concentration upon the most personal details of her life and her relationships? There is a type of delicious outrage, or so television and the press would have us believe, that fills the public's collective breast when a woman betrays society by murdering. Although it is clear that women are much more likely to be victims, popular entertainment, both written and electronic, indicates that woman as killer is perversely alluring.

P.D. James commented that a constant remark made to her is, 'And what's a nice woman like you doing writing crime fiction . . .?' The implication is, of course, that 'nice' women are somehow too clean to besmirch themselves with fictional or actual crime. Such comments are the reflection of a constant, yet frequently subtle, stereotyping. In the media women are treated according to their perceived roles—a marketable personality in an attractive, well-groomed body, or as female fodder for infotainment. In *Lessons in Murder* and *Death Down Under*, I explored the relentless appetite our media has for 'human interest' stories. In our society, it is almost as if a road accident, a murder or a political scandal do not exist until they appear on the screen or, to a lesser extent, in the first few pages of a newspaper, preferably with a photograph. And this is not, for the individual, fame. It is very often the casual destruction of privacy, of dignity, as the media's practitioners probe the secrets of the victims, of the perpetrators, of their relatatives and friends.

In these domestic dramas, played out so depressingly every day in our media, women's desire for individuality and concomitant autonomy is rewarded with violence. But the world is changing, and these changes are reflected in our fiction. Writers such as Sue Grafton, Marcia Muller and Sara Paretsky in America, Liza Cody in Britain, and Marele Day in Australia, have created female protagonists who are in many ways critical of, and alienated from, their social milieux. These main characters are not the modern equivalents of Wentworth's Miss Silver or Christie's Miss Marple, both maiden ladies who were firmly part of their society and who observed, rather than took an active part in, the drama. No, these are modern women, making it the hard way in a harsh and often violent world, largely unprotected by males, and frequently finding them lethal opponents, or, as an ironic comment upon the traditional 'dames' of the hard-boiled male detective—sexual playthings.

Another reflection of our society is the rise of the female police officer. Once an adjunct to a male, directed to see to children and comfort the overwrought relative, women are now attaining higher ranks and functioning effectively within a still largely patriarchal organisation. My series character, Detective Inspector Carol Ashton, operates in a peculiar vacuum, largely surrounded by males, working for them and with them, yet apart—not only because of her gender, but because of her sexuality. Hiding her closeted gayness is yet another necessity in a world where women have to constantly compromise or, at least on the surface, play by the (male) rules. The dichotomy between Carol Ashton's profession, which is posited upon the destruction of privacy, both of victim and perpetrator, and her personal life, which is essentially based on deception and secrecy, presents an interesting conflict. This conflict between appearance and actuality is one familiar to many women who step outside the roles our society has constructed for them. For example, the failure of Lindy Chamberlain to successfully enact the role of distraught mother within the guidelines established by society and reinforced by the media, almost certainly encouraged authorities to charge her with the murder of her daughter.

Detective Inspector Carol Ashton is the main character in a series of crime novels. But she is more than this. She is also a means to explore many issues. Her gender alone in such a position of high authority in an organisation noted for its male bonding presents an interesting variation and is a source of disharmony. She is good-looking, and used by the police force in media liaison when particularly explosive political issues are involved. Has her physical attractiveness been important to her success? Would she have attained the same rank if she'd been ugly, or if the large male-dominated organisation hadn't had pressure to promote women to senior positions? Carol's high media profile means she's given cases where political pressures encourage fast results and tidy solutions. And there's the complication of her sexual orientation, which forces her into a double life that she believes is necessary to maintain her authority and career path.

Carol's efforts to juggle her personal life and her professional life, while at the same time convincing herself of the probity of exposing others' secrets although hiding her own, give opportunities to present the reader with a range of issues. It is easy to state one's position on moral questions when they are abstract ideas, but when flesh and blood is put upon them, and a character with whom the reader identifies brings to life the conflicts and moral ambiguities, then it is much harder to take an uncompromising stand and say, 'This is wrong and that is right.' Carol finds, as most of us do, that life is situation ethics, where the struggle is to balance one's conscience against pragmatic considerations.

In *Cop Out* Carol is presented with, as her sergeant tells her, 'an open and shut case'. A woman, reported by her husband as emotionally unstable, has apparently lost control and beaten her brother to death with a hammer. The stereotypes come into play immediately: she's a weak, erratic, hysterical woman, possibly crazed by drugs, who acted on impulse without any thought of the consequences. Her husband is blameless—he tried to help her by consulting a psychiatrist, but she is fatally flawed. Carol comes under considerable pressure to accept that view, and not to investigate further.

If women battle to break out of stereotypical roles, so do men. But male roles, both in reality and in fiction, are usually autonomous, powerful, and, ultimately, authoritarian. Men command their own destinies: women are expected to take into account the destinies of those around them—not to be 'selfish'. Surely, then, the ultimate in selfishness is the woman who kills for herself. Our society understands a woman who inveigles a man to murder on her behalf, but to do the deed herself is stepping rather too far outside the boundaries of her assigned role. Hence the media's (and society's) infatuation with this dangerous individual—she's dared to join the boys' games.

In general terms, women operate in subsidiary positions within our society, not having anything even approaching equality in the institutions that form its framework. There is no parity of representation—not in politics, law, finance, business, sport, entertainment, information services, religion—and certainly not in the commission on criminal offences. But there *is* one area where women have equality. The writing of crime fiction.

There is something that the feminine approach can bring to

crime, both in life and in fiction. We see our society fragmenting as the gulf between have and have-not widens. Violence is part of entertainment, whether it be stylised on a screen, ritualised in print or part of our daily diet of news. The rise of the serial killer, the achievement of particularly hideous crimes, often by packs of men (women rarely, if ever, hunt in packs . . . yet) and the cynical acceptance of graft and corruption are characteristics of a rabid society whose excesses are fed and fuelled by the sensationalism of the media. Crime fiction, devoured by so many readers, is a means not only to entertain, but to question given certainties, to present alternatives, to create positive role models, to explore the where, when, how, who—and, most importantly—the *why*.

Women who write crime fiction may yet be the ultimate subversives. The shock troops of feminists come and go, the backlash swells, but, ignoring the tumult, nice women sit down to typewriters and word processors and create deceptions . . .

JAN McKEMMISH

Jan McKemmish was born at Tongala, Victoria, in 1950. She is the author of the spy novel A Gap in the Records *(Sybylla Press, 1985),* Only Lawyers Dancing *(Angus&Robertson, 1992) and several prose and performance pieces. She is currently working on her third novel.*

Reliable Pleasures

JAN McKEMMISH

When I try to speak or write about crime fiction I run into all sorts of trouble and become incoherent, contradictory, over-serious, flippant and stupid. And I do not achieve resolution. I am ambivalent.

Crime fiction is play: the play of the reader with the known narrative; the play of the writer with the body of work that is the entire genre; the play of words, with the vernacular fictions we imagine in our law abiding lives to be the tongue of the illegal. The corpse in this case is the body of work. The mystery is not who did it, but why, and why women. And like a good detective story this is a false mystery. Women have always written popular fiction. What is interesting is the appearance of so many doing it at this time

For myself it is not a mystery. Going to the popular genres is a way of going out of the woman writing category, to visit themes and ideas that deal beyond the personal, the domestic, the first person biographical. It is irritating that the category 'women writers' continues to be used. I aquiesce.

We pursue the fictional criminal without special pleading,
the truth is all
and we are all suspect until the clever man appears,

armed with his questions
his integrity
and his private drives, like neurosis, a special case of
aloneness, a murdered wife or a fall from grace with leaves his
body, his physical prowess, that caress, his willingness, in
tact.[1]

Perhaps women are turning again to the writing of crime fiction not just for the money or the readership (we write to be read; many people read crime fiction; it is possible to write a decent crime novel, people do it all the time; it is not essential to always be writing great literature; people are more likely to buy a crime novel than an obscure exercise in avant-garde feminism or postmodernism; publishers like them, they think they will sell), but because crime fiction insists on being both/and, domestic and social, personal and public.

I am willing, now, with fake integrity and a career that pays
to look at the business, investigation, (as fiction),
retrospection
stories told backwards to deceive and satisfy[2]

There are only so many novels to be written about adultery, how could you, I suffer, mother. The detective travels, acts, talks smart, has access, these things are all narratively attractive. And the detective works. This is particularly narratively attractive to writing women characters who, traditionally, conventionally, do not, or do not primarily, work.

telling stories that have no history
this I would argue is the essence
repetition and ahistoricism
simulating urban realism with fast talk and late nights, booze
and cigarettes, dancing to the back beat and moving like statues

in the twilight,
pleasuring you.[3]

In a recent discussion with some women who were researching the whole question of women detectives and crime fiction we struck on the idea that the female detective, heroic, tough, able to look after herself, is a sort of fantasy of how women have to be every day of their working lives, facing casual mysogyny, sexism, the banality of it all, keeping the domestic together, of having to go on year in year out reminding, nagging, putting up with, picking up after. The liquid contempt of the general male (as opposed to the general niceness of the specific male) is like soil erosion in our soul.

I drink and smoke, still,
that sort of living dangerously without romance,
the attraction of the continuous present
that's something you should know before you begin.
I am not morally defensible in the codes and styles of the end of
the century, I am a suppliant of the past, an Australian, an
amnesiac, believer of easy myths and silences, still.[4]

It was probably no accident that there was a boom in publishing crime fiction in Australia in the 1980s, a time renowned for an actual boom in criminal, illegal, immoral and undetectable, unpunishable crimes. While we readers and writers played fantastic games with detectives and their individual quests, the whole social fabric moved west with a vengeance, pursuing the mighty dollar, living higher and higher, squandering economic reform on the green baize knowledge of too complicated to catch. Clever dicks.

And does the fashion for serial murderers hide the statistics: most murders are domestic, husbands, wives, children? Like the fashion for vampires, hiding the more ordinary horrors of sexual power games, incest, rape, dying.

> *I did these things for my own reasons, family secrets, work,*
> *people I have met and liked and seen disappear, like smoke.*
> *I stir the ashes and do not know what I am keeping alive.*[5]

If, as the old arguments go, we need a national literature to give ourselves back to ourselves, to know who we are, perhaps we needed crime fiction to give us a rest from the blatant uncertainties of the newspaper trails of criminality and public corruption, the NSW police for example, a sort of social and moral retirement from the battle. It is no accident, I suspect, that the stuff of early 1980s investigative journalism disappeared, appearing to dissolve into a taste for crime fiction.

> *I repeat the stories, of corruption, investigation, resolution,*
> *retribution, of mourning, which could be any newspaper stories in*
> *any city after Hiroshima, Vietnam, pure capitalism, the*
> *Rainbow Warrior.*
> *The years of the rich, I say, becoming pompous,*
> *wanting there to be meaning in the talk.*
> *I say, we can mourn the deaths, the decline of social sense,*
> *without it being nostalgic. It takes about seven years.*[6]

The narratives that investigate the simpler rhertorics of crime fiction are various, sometimes problematic, often repetitious, and ultimately about pleasure. The pleasure first of intellectual activity, the puzzle, the solution, away from the cloying domestic and the clawing romances. Cool. Social. In the world. A little surprised. Not ladylike.

> *We took the boat out for a practice in Black Wattle Bay, it was*
> *an aluminium runabout, two stroke, a set of oars, put put put*
> *across to the fish markets and back. Fine.*
> *We put it on the top of the car and drove across the city to*
> *Solange's place and stowed it under the trees near the jetty.*

*Up at her house we sat at the water-view-windows and
drank coffee and ate steak sandwiches, waiting for the dark. It
began to rain, the harbour disappeared into the rain sweeping in
great drives and movements, we watched the rain. The rain
stopped. It was dark. Low cloud. No stars. We put on our all-
blacks and Frances produced two balaclavas, navy blue army
disposal numbers, and we slid the boat into the water and
rowed out to the end of the jetty, the motor sputtered to life and
we moved into the darkness.*

*Robert's house was high above the harbour edge, we cut the
motor too far out and had to row in, fumbling and lurching off
into circles of uneven stroke, shouting in whispers and sweating
with the effort of pulling, we realised, against a tide going out
laden with storm water. We landed three houses down, soaked
with our own exertion, balaclavas are bloody hot.*[7]

I have often said that detective fiction is essentially a conservative
form; the ritual of resolution, the expectations of the reader. It
is these elements of the reading process that provide the reliable
pleasures, we can relax into the other-world details of the fiction,
relishing, wallowing, aghast, knowing in the end all will be revealed,
order restored. When we read detective fiction we are always
rereading. And while the recent interventions of left and feminist
detectives mean that less conservative material/content is
present—collectives, fascists, bad doctors, corrupt public
officials—these are differences in degree rather than substance. The
structures of the narrative remain the same.

I am not convinced by this argument. Crime fiction as a genre
has always been aware of its social content, context and literary
intent. Dashiell Hammet, the populariser of the American hard-
boiled style of detective, was interested in several political issues
and the politics of writing: the nature of urban capitalism, the
divergence morally between the rich and the ordinary, the creation
of an urban American vernacular to stand against the hegemonic

'English literature' that had dominated American literary aesthetics. And he was not alone, Dos Pasos, Hemingway, Faulkner, Stein and Fitzgerald were all working away from the English and towards the American at the same time.

I write off social practices that concern me and that includes other writing, as social practice, which indeed it is.

I write to disturb. I am generally disturbed by the world, even when it is going well. Life is a melange of mysteries. Doctor Freud et al have created mysteries for each of us. Mystery is perhaps the theme of the twentieth century, information, versions, cover-ups and revelations, files and conspiracies, paranoid rumours years later become matters of fact, our heroines become police informers, are we shocked at our willingness to be deceived?

Writing in relation to genre can be both limitation and freedom. Like the reading experience it is safe, I can lean against the conventions. I am propped up by the bodies. I can push against the limitations, making a small space for myself, investigating what is possible.

To put it another way, I have a weakness for cliche. I have turned this weakness into awareness and a sort of ironic play that, with a bizarre imagination and a willingness to push things through cliche and into context or consequences, manages to produce a sort of immediately familiar but slightly disturbing popular fiction, I mimic the voices of the master narrative, the ancestors, I copy and change, I use grabbed ideas, current phrases, a sort of fake veracity of tone and voice is achieved by appearing to be resonant.

her face against mine, slightly, lightly, as the touch of a moth
passing you at your desk in the night, the reading lamp on, on
its way to the flame.[8]

Genre is a body of work in the process of constant change and referring both to itself and to its social conditions. This is a simple knowledge but one that allows a great deal of writing to be done fairly easily: he had a gun, it was a Smith and Wesson; he had a typewriter, it was a Smith Corona. My bias is towards the American, Hammet, Chandler, Leonard, Didion, Dos Pasos: she had a computer, an Apple Mac. But I am writing in Australia, in Sydney, here and now, or then and now, I am interested in the ways we can represent our society in generic terms, how the genre is altered and changed by our realities of crime and espionage, our place in the world, our history in relation to violence, to images of criminality, to economies of the illegal.

One of the freedoms of crime fiction is that all sorts of obsessions and knowledges can find a place, as scenery, as padding, as diversion from the main journey.

She reads too many novels, I think again, as I leave another plaintive message on her answer phone and wait for her to not ring me back.

I despair of ever being able to speak.

I leave another message on the answer phone, 'am being pursued by a gang of slave traders, must talk to you immediately.'

And another, 'have contracted rare tropical virus and have only weeks to live, please call.'

And finally, 'see you've got a new client, he's on my files, have several photographs of your mate, you might like to telephone me soonest' and took the phone off the hook. She turned up at midnight, virtually panting with what I took to be excitement but which turned out to be terror.

'How can you live in this suburb, it scares me to death just getting out of a cab,' she says.

I look at her, is this the person I wanted to bare my soul to. 'What are you talking about?' I say with all the words inflected. 'Redfern,' she says, 'how can you live in Redfern, it's so violent.' I take her up to the second floor and make a cup of tea and stand her on the balcony and I say, 'see that tower block over there, what does it say?'

> 'T.N.T.' she reads.
> 'And what's that building over there?'
> 'The brewery, the university, the newspaper.'
> 'Right,' I say, 'see?'
> She doesn't see. That it's in somebody's interest to have everyone
> think Redfern is a dangerous place to live. The house I am
> living in, renting, will be sold up the market three times in three
> years, tripling in price, there will be BMWs and Rolls Royces
> living in the street soon, not just passing through to collect the
> rents and payoffs.[9]

A sort of freedom. We may divert, we may enjoy, but we must also be responsible and return to the task at hand, which is pleasure, intimacy, peeping into people's lives while they are in (ludicrous) crisis. The sheer absurdity of the plots, often, the cleverness, all these things remove us from the messiness of murder, and give us a thrill: vicariously we visit, for a moment, the psychopath, the greedy, the stupid. For fictional crime stories are rarely about domestic violence or random violence or anger, they are rarely about the power of violence, to intimidate, to force, to have power over. They are more often about money, about scams, about trying on something all of us after a bad day at the bank would cheerfully like to invest in.

And in the more sophisticated forms of Ruth Rendell and Patricia Highsmith, they are about character, madness, alcoholism, dysfunction, venality and obsessions, ruthlessness. We have all been there or somewhere like it. And the popular aspect of popular fiction is part of this pleasure. The books come out fast, they are bought, read, passed around, they are almost devoured. What is intriguing about contemporary crime fiction is the precarious achievement: will they (re)present enough of what we know about the current world plus the strange, the new, the dangerous, for us to be satisfied? In its very contemporaneity crime fiction plays a difficult game, to deliver evolutions and disruptions of a society's shifting images of romance, sex and violence while reproducing the safety of resolution and justice.

And while there are these serious edges to the genre, its art is in absurdity (plot); exaggeration (character); constraint (resolution); and language, the spin of the phrase, fabulous fast-lane dialogue, all the things you wished you'd thought to say at the time; allowed humour; flights of purple and blood red, seduction and pleasure, honesty and sentimentality, the sex and violence nexus.

> *He looks at me and laughs with relief. 'You don't care,' he says, almost disbelieving that his story has failed to move me.*
> *'No,' I say, 'I don't. Kitchens and heat. Fire and burns. I'd probably like it better if you told me he bobbed to the surface and suffered for an hour or two, his life crawling slowly before his eyes, his half-a-head aching with an unspeakable pain and his legs being wrenched from his body by sharks and the car engines tied to his feet.' I'm leaning towards drunk as I say this and am immediately sorry. The things you don't know you think until they come out of your mouth.*
> *'You read too much Robert Ludlum,' he says.*
> *I say, 'I never read books. Did they fuck the girls before or after?'*
> *Silence. Not even a look. Going too far.*[10]

There is a difference between publishing with a small feminist press and with a large multinational. It feels different for a start. You know that you are not, with Murdoch, involved in changing anything, the text becomes a matter of you and the reader, it is all you can do. With *A Gap In The Records* the production of the book was part of the narrative, to see if a feminist press would take a pop novel, to see if they would take one that didn't mention the word feminism, to see if the collective editing process would work (it did), to see if the book would get any attention at all (it did), to see if some small thing could be shifted.

When I sat down to write *Only Lawyers Dancing* I did so because I was interested in the way violent crimes work across our lives, how this can be represented, how this can be done, entertainingly, without a single heroic detective, who, by her singularity, her victory over, relieves us all of responsibility. Although most detectives have offsiders, helpers, secretaries, handy mates in the police department, it is the detective, alone and driven, who carries the job of morality and of justice. In *Only Lawyers Dancing* I chose two narrators to immediately deal with the problem (as I saw it) of this heroic alienated individual. By using two voices, two narrators, two characters, I could immediately disrupt this imperative and play with the ripple effects of duality, doubling, complicating, difference, and, in terms of plot and character, I could play with the ideas of trust, veracity, relationship. As a feminist I could attempt to represent women in relation to culture and to each other, part of rather than apart from. Anne Stevens and Frances Smith play out a scenario of friendship which is brittle, terse, tough, confronting and as solid as a rock. I like that a lot. I too have my romantic moments.

These days we do not write only in relation to other (fiction) writing. Journalism, history, science, TV, film, radio, these texts carry the signs of literature back and forth: few fiction writers do only that for a living or as the only sort of writing they do.

In *A Gap In The Records* I used postcards and maps as agents to the text. In *Only Lawyers Dancing* I used descriptions of slide photographs and a sort of film-obsessed visually-drenched prose. There were two or three intentions to this. The slides for me are period devices recalling the 1950s and 60s family technologies of memory. The idea came to me from a John Berger and Jean Mohr book, *Another Way of Telling* (Granta Books, 1989).

The drenched prose was an attempt to colour the film noir dominance of the crime genre (more perfectly achieved of course on film, see Martin Scorceses' *Cape Fear*) and to represent and disrupt some of the recent constructions of Sydney as Chicago/Los

Angeles/America and Melbourne as London or Paris. It is no accident that the really successful crims in *Only Lawyers Dancing* come from Melbourne.

And the device was intent on another level—memory, the past, ordinary lives. In moving away from the authority of the lone detective, I wanted to explore the legitimacy of characters with histories, contexts, family and friends, ambitions, ambivalence, jobs, domestic realms and lives containing ideas, lived within culture, not outside it. In this way it is a sort of social realist project which ends up as a sort of hyper-realist prose using the cliches of fictional criminality and the realisms of memory, family, work, place and friendship.

Just after *Only Lawyers Dancing* came out I had a phone call from a journalist on a rural newspaper. He had read the book and recognised some of the scenery and some of the plot. We had several conversations about the original crimes the novel drew on, how it dealt with them and whether this was ethical, sensitively done, useful. He told me there had been a book written about this material and I found it recently in a secondhand bookshop. It is a heartbreaking and gruelling account of domestic violence, child abuse, rape and murder. I am both glad and sorry I did not come across it before I wrote the novel. Sorry because these terrible stories should be widely known, but ultimately glad because the (terrible) real does not lend itself to the neat and pleasurable play of crime fiction and the humour and fake heroics that requires.

> . . . *we stepped outside, into the rain and the darkness of the trees. As the garden lights came on the dogs bounded past us to the house, we were gone, staggering with exhaustion, flying down the steps in the cliff and into the boat. It was half filled with water and bits of meat come loose from the dogs' stash floated in the mire. We rowed, rather wildly and the rain came down just then, washing the stench of sweat and blood out into the harbour. We rowed out into the storm, thunder, lightning, it*

would be just our luck to be struck, after all that. The tide was
coming in now and I fixed on the faint wink of the Harbour
Bridge and let the boat drift, the motor wouldn't start and I
was grateful for the deep silence within the sound of the storm,
the curtains of rain flinging themselves down just for us. It was
so dark and featureless we could have ended up anywhere and
did, two bays down from Solange's jetty. We struggled up
through a park and huddled in the doorway of some shops at
Edgecliff. I prised the ten dollar bill from my bra and we hailed
a taxi, Stevens fell into it with the sort of relief that is so deep it
is indescribable. She stared at me all the way to Number 15,
Ithaca Road and I gritted my teeth and bit my lip, holding back
the laughter that would soon become hysterical and make the
driver remember us. We got out at the corner and headed off
into the opposite direction watching the taxi off into the rain, the
streets were running rivers and we waded down towards the
black harbour and fell on Solange's door bell. Laughing now,
blubbering and weeping and gasping for breath, so much held in,
so much silence. Stevens raced straight to the bathroom and
vomited. I took all my clothes off in the hallway, leaving them
heaped and puddling, grabbed a towel from the bathroom and a
blanket from the spare bed, I wrapped my head in the towel
and my body in the blanket and said, 'Tea', to Solange's surreal
polite questions, it was as if we had been to another planet and
back and no time had passed. The storm swept the water
outside the windows, battering against the glass, to come in and
get us. I pressed my face to the glass and dared it. The thunder
sounded right overhead and I fell to the floor, dare the gods and
they will respond.[11]

I make fiction as a construction. An accumulation of styles and
voices, ways of telling, representing. This approach to making a
text is partly about refusing the God-like qualities of writing, to
make the writing exist, beyond and despite the narrative, refusing

the constraints and comforts of narrative closure. I do it because I like that sort of writing myself and I like to be able to see how writers distance themselves from the text, how we can allow the text to exist, to be seen as fiction, while doing all the seductions fictions do. This too is play but it is also a bit serious about the politics of narrative. What you say is informed by how you say it, what it is possible to say is affected by the techniques of saying. These are not simple issues, and they are not easy. If they were easy and sayable we would not write whole novels investigating the possibilities.

NOTES

1. *Outakes* (unpublished deletions), from Jan McKemmish, *Only Lawyers Dancing*, Collins Angus & Robertson, Sydney, 1992
2. *Outakes*, Ref 1. continued
3. *Outakes*, Ref 1. continued
4. *Outakes*, Ref 1. continued
5. *Outakes*, Ref 1. continued
6. *Outakes*, Ref 1. continued
7. *Outakes*
8. *Outakes*
9. *Outakes*
10. *Only Lawyers Dancing*, p. 62
11. *Outakes*, Ref 7. continued

KERRY GREENWOOD

Kerry Greenwood was born in the Melbourne suburb of Footscray, and still lives there. She has written a number of plays, including The Troubadours *with Stephen D'Arcy, worked as a director, producer, folk singer and costume-maker. Her first book,* Cocaine Blues, *was published by McPhee/Gribble in 1989, her second* Flying Too High *in 1990, her third* Murder on the Ballarat Train *in 1991, her fourth* Death at Victoria Dock *in 1992 and her fifth* The Screen Hill Murder *in 1993, all featuring the stylish flapper sleuth, Phryne Fisher. She is currently working on her fifth Phryne Fisher book. When she is not writing, she is a locum solicitor for the Legal Aid Commission and unpaid curator of a menagerie including four cats and a duck called Son of Quark.*

She has no children, and lives with a Registered Wizard.

Phyrne Fisher

K E R R Y   G R E E N W O O D

When the charming Hilary McPhee, to whom I can refuse nothing, asked me to write two books for McPhee/Gribble, I decided to try and create a female hero. This was going to be my first published book, and I was not going to waste the opportunity, as I didn't know if it would ever occur again.

I have been reading detective stories since my first encounter with Arséne Lupin and Sherlock Holmes at about ten years of age, and I thought I was familiar with the genre and that I understood how it worked. What I was familiar with was the way that men write detective stories, which is not the same as the way I do it; and I gave a lot of extra work to my long-suffering and patient editor, Sophie Cunningham, while I learned to write a mystery.

I think I have got the elements of the skill now.

I can't write about the present. I am a Duty Solicitor with the Legal Aid Commission; what they call in New South Wales a Public Defender. The job entails turning up at a Magistrate's Court and representing everyone who does not have a solicitor. Consequently, whenever I am on an escalator in a shopping centre and see those posters which demand 'Have you seen these men?' I always have. They are my clients, as is every drug addict hanging out for a fix, every beaten wife and sexually abused child, every shoplifter and car thief and credit card defrauder and heartbroken parent of a suicidal girl; all of the lost, the miserable, the hard-done-by, the strange, and the completely bonkers who happen to be wherever I am.

This is not a job where once can bear much more realism.

It has dawned upon me that the writers of all the mean streets genre have never been part of them. In the gutter, one requires stars, not more shit. I love being a Duty Solicitor, I am good at it, and nothing exceeds the sense of achievement as one leaves the court, with all one's free (if chastened) clients, and no one has gone to jail who could possibly be rescued. But I cannot write about it. Really I can't. Writing is my escape from the real world. Therefore I needed a historical period to write about.

A long time ago, I was at Melbourne University, doing Legal History. It was necessary to do some original research, from documents, and the rest of my middle-class compatriots were going to search the family archives for something entitled 'My Grandfather the Judge'. I did not have this option as my grandfather was a carpenter, and my father is a wharfie. However, as I was casting about for an angle, I realised that 1928 was a year in which all sorts of interesting repressive legislation had been passed to do down the unions, and I could ask the Waterside Workers' Federation to let me look at their archives, since Daddy was a member in good standing even though he had gone on to be a foreman. I wrote to the federation and they agreed, and because this was the first original research I had ever done, I overdid it. I read all the newspapers for that year. I talked to all the old wharfies I could find about the 1928 strike and anything else they wanted to tell me. I went to Canberra and spent a frozen, miserably lonely week ferreting through the archives. I knew an awful lot about 1928 by the time I had finished.

So I thought again about 1928 and did some more research. Interesting times. Women, forced to work during the war, stayed in the workforce. They were practicing law, and medicine, and flying planes and driving cars. Air-race records were held by women. The Queen Victoria Hospital was staffed by women and paid for by every woman in Victoria contributing her shilling. And they had cut off their hems and their hair and were taking on anything and everything, and did not even seem to notice the severe leaders in the papers insisting that they were Going Too Far.

1928, I thought, ideal year for the female hero I was going to create. I needed a name. Psyche, they said. Too pure. Psyche was a maiden of great virtue before Eros got to her. I looked up the birth notices for 1900, when she would have been born. Greek names were popular; Iris, Irene, Psyche, and—aha—Phryne. I knew about Phryne from my favourite Ancient Greek historian and gossip, Herodotus. Phryne was a courtesan, who was of such surpassing beauty that her counsel, when her case was going against her, stripped off her garment and displayed her naked to the court, asking rhetorically 'Could anyone this beautiful have done anything illegal?' And the jury, of course, acquitted her. This was the Phryne who offered to rebuild the walls of Thebes, if she could put on them a sign: 'The walls of Thebes, ruined by time, rebuilt by Phryne the courtesan'. The citizens had preferred their ruins. Oh, yes, Phryne was a good name. More research and I found that it was a common 1920s newspaper convention for 'lady of light repute'. Perfect. Phyrne (pronounced 'Fry-knee'; that is not how the ancient Greeks would have said it, but it was how the twentieth century said it, two long e's, as in Irene and Iris). Then I wanted a really symbolic last name; Fisher for the Roi Pécheoneur, the sinner/fisher King from the Grail legend; and also for a notorious street in 1920s Paris, the Rue de la Chat-qui-Péche, the Street of the Fishing Cat. Phryne Fisher.

I examined the concept of a hero, and read the literature of the time. She had to be a hero in 1920s mode, not a modern hero, should such a thing exist. To write a successful historical novel it is essential that the character match the time. Phryne is a 1920s woman, born in 1900, and her concerns and her mind must be of the right period.

What sort of hero was a 1920s hero?

Back to the papers. Airmen were heroes, so were daring young men who climbed mountains and boldly went where no one had gone before. John Buchan (a much under-appreciated writer) had a clever, nervous, intelligent hero, and a big brawny strong hero; Sandy Arbuthnot and Richard Hannay. Dorothy Sayers invented the shell-shocked, honourable, determined hero; Lord Peter Wimsey. Agatha Christie invented the foreign and slightly comic hero with the funny accent; Hercule Poirot (even the name is pear-shaped); and Leslie Charteris invented Simon Templar, the Saint.

Hmm. Much as I liked Buchan, I could not imagine a blocky, Hannay-like female hero; not that there could not be one, but just that I could not imagine it. I wanted the 'nerves and nose' of Wimsey and of Sandy Arbuthnot, but I also wanted my female hero to be strong, a good role-model, and nerves would interfere with that. I could not see myself getting away with a stock character like Poirot, nor did he fire my imagination, since I did not like either him or his dim offsider. I note in passing that Watson, Holmes's partner, is not stupid; it is just that Holmes is so blindingly intelligent.

Not a female in any of the books, except the redoubtable Harriet Vane, to use. I admire Sayers's creation of Harriet Vane. She has guts, intelligence, and force. But she always has to have Peter Wimsey to come in and rescue her; she makes her first appearance as a victim; and standing alone she always gets into trouble from which she has to be extracted. The relationship between Harriet and Lord Peter is, on the other hand, the only one I know of in literature which treats of honour and equality of power between a man and a woman; as such it is revolutionary, and deserves to be studied.

But not by me. The Saint, I thought, well, what about the Saint? I had read all of the huge output of Leslie Charteris, buying books from op shops as I always did because I could not afford new books. The Saint is period—the first Saint book was written in 1928. He is a very attractive character. Clever, ruthless, good-looking, with black hair and blue eyes, a good fighter, a witty talker, with a talent for trouble. James Bond without the sexism, Sapper without the anti-Semitism and racism which makes him so hard to bear. And Charteris writes a very good plot. In the first book, *Meet the Tiger*, a female associate of the Saint, Patricia Holm, is introduced. She climbs walls and handles guns and is brave and quick-witted, though, of course, she also needs to be rescued. I would create a female Saint, who would not need to be rescued.

So I created Phryne Fisher; black hair and green eyes, dresses like a *Vogue* cover, fast with a gun and a degree in streetfighting; born very poor and becomes very rich. I made her poor to begin with so that she could really appreciate wealth; I gave her enough money to be able to do anything she liked and a period in history where it was possible for women to do whatever they liked without incurring social ruin. I made her aristocratic so that social forces should not daunt her; and fashionably beautiful so that she would have every weapon to be a hero.

Then I sat back and watched her go into action.

It was a strange process. Now she is so real that I would not be surprised to meet her in the street. I distinctly remember creating her, with all the attributes of a hero; now she shocks me. I am not ruthless in the way Phryne is ruthless; I have never shot anyone in my life, and I don't think that I could.

Phryne can.

Like the Saint, she operates outside the law, police procedures, and social expectations. Like Wimsey, her most useful weapon is her intelligence. Like Sandy Arbuthnot, she is quick and intuitive. Like all detective heroes, she stands for justice. I don't know if there is a General Theory of Detective Stories Written by Women. The form of such a story has always struck me as important. Detective stories put a nice neat framework of moral and social forces over the messy, bloody, endlessly fascinating subject of murder. Everyone is interested in murder, and no one likes to admit it. The subject is obscene in the way that sex used to be. Death, it is said, is the ultimate obscenity, and the process of taking onto oneself the awesome responsibility of taking life away is fascinating. But no one wants to admit it, or there would be a greater sale of Coroner's Reports than there is. The detective story serves two purposes: it sanitises murder, and it provides a form in which the reader can respectably indulge what is seen as an obscene interest in violent death. I have never heard anyone (except me) say that they are endlessly absorbed in murder, but lots of people boast that they have read the whole output of Agatha Christie.

That being so, I needed to do several things with the Phryne books. One was to make sure that no one, however minor a character, ended up dead without due notice being taken of their humanity. I have read far too many books, especially American ones, where people are blasted off the face of the earth merely as a plot mechanism, and without even a small note to say that, as Douglas Adams says, they had other things to do with their day than to get murdered. I also needed to avoid the mean streets and similar pitfalls of attempting to get my effect by describing in full and gory detail what happens, say, to a motorcycle rider who hits a chain-link fence at 100 miles an hour and is strained through it eyeball by eyeball. I also needed to avoid the 'psychopath as hero' theme so prevalent in books like *The Silence of the Lambs*, which I know to be entirely untrue. I have met, in my profession, more psychopaths than is really consistent with a comfortable life, and they aren't like that. There are no Night Stalkers swollen with power; just pathetic little monsters with their dreams of blood and their aspirations to be someone. Dylan Thomas, a great reader of mean streets books, relates in his *Letter from America* that he went hunting the great Chicago auk . . . 'and I found a little Brooklyn sparrow, twittering for crumbs and buddies'.

So. I also had to invent, or discover, a set of ethics for my female hero. Are there different ethics for women? What about sex? What about love?

I solved them by just writing the book and seeing how it came out.

Phryne is for justice, but not necessarily for law. She will fix the situation, producing the required and just result, but not by legal means. She bribed a child molester to confess by offering him the services, in the death cell, of a whore who specialises in appearing prepubertal (*Flying Too High*). With her associates, she will entrap a cocaine dealer (*Cocaine Blues*), or a murderer (*Murder on the Ballarat Train*), using herself, if necessary, as bait. In *Death at Victoria Dock* she abrogates to herself the ultimate authority which gave James Bond his title, and shoots two men, in the back. In *The Screen Hill Murder* she returns blackmail photographs to the victim.

The real (sexual politics) objection to James Bond and his ilk is that the lovers are cardboard replicas. They are female automatons, with no reality, no freedom of action, and no will. Phryne's lovers, all of whom are very attractive, are real people. She likes them. She treats them well. She makes love to them with erotic flair, skill, and without breaking any hearts or getting herself entangled in dreary emotional bonds. I expected, when I designed Phryne to be promiscuous in the most benevolent sense, in the same way as all those male heroes are, to be much criticised by women readers, who would be shocked. This has not proved to be the case. Women love to read of a woman who does not find it necessary to fall in love, to pine, to wait for the telephone to ring, to fall pregnant, or conversely to become hard or unsusceptible to male charm. I am personally entirely susceptible to male charm. I like men, mostly. The only criticism I have had about the lovers comes from two sources: a radical lesbian group who are opposed to the introduction of men into feminist novels at all, and some men who find Phryne threatening because she does not care about men in the way that she should. I have discounted both views in my writing, because I consider that men are essential, however much they may annoy or appal me, and anyone who does not like my books is under no compulsion to read them.

Besides, the lovers are needed for the plot. Sometimes they are part of the way Phryne finds things out: Lindsay in *Murder on the Ballarat Train*. Sometimes they are central to the plot, as the reason why she gets into the situation: Peter Smith in *Death at Victoria Dock* and Sasha in *Cocaine Blues*. They are not all young and cute. Sometimes, I admit, they are a mere distraction, like Dr Mark in *Flying Too High*. However, I write to amuse, not instruct, though I can sneak a fair bit of instruction past under my reader's guard. Women, for whom I mainly write as far as I write for anyone, enjoy escapism, they like Phryne to be free to take lovers and to leave them, like they enjoy her baths and her Rose de Geuldy perfume, her clothes and her car.

So I made her rich and I made her free, and she proceeded to take over the books. I have very little control over how the plot goes, after the initial idea. I do not know who the murderer is; I do not know the solution to the mystery (if I do think I know, I am quite often proved wrong). I set up the situation at the start of the book, an immediate and sudden shock; shots shattering the windscreen, chloroform leaking into the first-class carriage. Then it is up to Phryne to decide what she will do to extract herself alive and then solve the problem. I often type all night in order to find out what is going to happen.

I do a lot of research, to place myself as far as it is possible in the 1920s. The crimes were the same, the concerns and social situation similar. World history is cyclic; the present world situation closely resembles 1910, and I have hopes that if we can avoid the First World War we may go on. The 1920s strangely resembled the early 1970s, which is when Australia got what was the *annus mirabilis*, 1968, in America. Therefore, I am not surprised to find free love, experimental marriage, contraception, new music, new theatre, drug fiends, and trouble in the Balkans.

I immerse myself in papers, causing my friends to enquire whether I am nesting. I then undertake something major in the house renovation line, like tearing up carpets, or stripping the door, and wait for an idea to hit.

Then I type all day and all night until the book is finished. It takes about six weeks, allowing for Legal Work and getting stuck at chapter seven. I am now familiar with my genre and my own writing style. I never have a second draft any more.

In style, I adopt a rather brittle, Noel Coward-ish form, using long sentences (my editor once sent me a sheet covered in dots, which she said was an emergency shipment of full stops). I send up the mean streets genre. My use of narrative style is unusual; the narrator has a dry and verbal wit as well as the character. This makes the books fun to read, and cuts down the amount of description. It is always useful, if one has to describe, say, a room, or the view from a window, to give the subject to a character, or two characters, to describe, so that one can pack into a small scene the characters' relation and reaction to each other and the subject, and so the reader gets a lot more information than they would otherwise get from a simple narrator's view.

This is like juggling eggs, but it is excellent when it works.

So there we have her; Phryne Fisher, female hero, free, rich, intelligent, loving, ruthless, educated, and attended by two communist taxi drivers and her devoted maid Dot, Mr and Mrs Butler, and two adopted daughters. She has no constraints upon her but those of time, place, and gravity, and she is clever, merciful, beautiful, and a great fighter for Order and Justice.

A hard job, but someone has to do it.

FINOLA MOORHEAD

Finola Moorhead was born in 1947 in Victoria, wrote her first

published poem in 1965 and became a professional writer in 1973,

after being chosen one of the playwrights to participate in the first

Australian National Playwrights' Conference. She was widely

published in magazines in the 70s and anthologies in the 80s. In 1980

she was Writer in Residence at Monash University. In 1985, two

books, Quilt, a Collection of Prose, *and* A Handwritten Modern

Classic *were published. In 1987,* Remember the Tarantella, *her first*

novel, and in 1991, Still Murder, *her second novel, were published.*

Still Murder *won the Vance Palmer Fiction Prize in the 1991*

Victorian Premier's Literary Awards.

Equal Writes

FINOLA MOORHEAD

Some are agonising about girlfriends and the amazing drama of coming out as a dyke or not in the police department. Some are such anti-woman women I recoil at their snobbery. Some are so butch, feminism might never have happened to lesbians. Some are so coy, their sexual proclivities never enter the story. Some are so heterosexual, they beg you to imagine that a woman can lead as promiscuous a life as Sam Spade and enjoy it. Some are funny, some are gutsy, some brave and some even think out their detection, which is truly the essence of the mystery genre. There are a lot of women writing mysteries these days.

If written by lesbians, the lesbians are not feminist, if written by 'feminists', the women aren't lesbian. Here are all these talented women, with their computers and the commitment to write and (they must have) the knowledge unearthed in the 1960s, 1970s and early 1980s by women and about women, and they're ignoring it. Why are the majority of these works devoid of feminist thought?

Still Murder is not a genre novel. It can't be, because it has a women-identified central reality.

But first, genre, what is genre? I'm aware of its meaning in practice, yet not comfortable with its etymology. Thinking of the word, 'genus': type/style with common structural characteristics?

Whodunit and how. Murder? A detective, amateur or professional. A small group of people, suspects. A locality. A puzzle.

Thinking of genre in painting helps a little: scenes from ordinary life. But it wasn't ordinary, was it? It was the bourgeois having pictures on their walls of happy peasants.[1] The peasants don't know they're art. Their aesthetic values would be quite different. I am sure they would have much preferred to have been portrayed clean, having wiped the melon juice from their chins, displaying what *they* had achieved or how hard it was to achieve, and thus grace the walls of the burghers' houses with their truth within the frame.

The irony is in the definition before we even start.

Scenes from ordinary life can hardly describe literary genre as it has evolved into works which conform to a certain pattern. Works which revolve on the axis of formula, turn on the spindle of suspense, play on the board or court with rules and skills for the entertainment of others, works in which a logical outcome always prevails. The attraction of the genre is in that common structural characteristic, the frame.

Such logical outcomes don't happen in ordinary life. What strikes most women about the world we live in is how stupidly it is operated politically. How most decisions by the power brokers are the worst possible solutions in the given situations, and wouldn't work in the logic of the mystery genre or even games. Obscene lack of reward for compassion or altruism prevails in our social and environmental reality. Unfortunately.

Genre fiction gives one relief from that; why ask why it is so popular? Little boxes of escape. Frames. A woman in her kitchen marks out a square where she is boss. This kitchen is like a symbol for other areas where a woman might exercise her intelligence. Bridge nights or golf days might be places where her skill can be executed too. Here she may pit herself against the sum of her talents in fair competition. Beyond the narrow boundaries of these spaces in time and place is a world governed by rules, rules which are largely hostile to her being autonomous and free, a regime which aggrieves her; 'reality'. Little boxes of logic and commonsense. Frames within which her virtue or virtuosity is confined are the only places where a woman might have control of circumstances.

Following the fight of the suffragettes in the early twentieth century for the vote and entrance into the professions, there was a great era of female detective fiction. The achievements of the feminists were enjoyed by the next generation, who for the most part did not maintain the fight against the patriarchal state. Rather, they internalised the victories into widening their own boundaries and expressing themselves. In the middle of the nineteenth century there was a mobilisation against the introduction of the Contagious Diseases Act, which also was followed by an era of women's genre writing. And earlier even still, if Mary Wollstonecraft's *A Vindication of the Rights of Woman* indicated a feminist era, then that period was followed by women writers in the gothic genre. If there's always been a women's movement (this century),[2] then it goes in waves of radical action and undulates into periods of reformism.

The continuum of women's thought and artistic production is constantly broken; it never really enters the debate in mainstream culture. Why was Matilda Joslyn Gage's analysis of women, church and state never studied in universities? If it were studied in the same way as say Adam Smith, or Marx even, imagine the understanding we would have by now of women, their position, their essence. I mean our. But even I slip into objectifying women. In genre novels, women's issues or feminist activities, such as rape crisis centres, are marginalised. They are not realised with the same credence that socialist theories are given in some strains of the genus. In this flood of women and lesbian detective writers I deduce little radical feminism. None attempt to change the basis of society,[3] or influence history and culture.

When the action's on the street, the mood of women's literature breaks into boundaries, experiments, spreads its form. One thinks of Virginia Woolf with her deep questions, *how can we influence history and culture?*, licking envelopes for the suffragettes. George Eliot no doubt admired the activities of Josephine Butler. I note that the French women were chaining themselves for the vote in 1935,[4] when the literary, lesbian artistic activity on the Left Bank was exciting. Our own wave of radical feminism saw its reflection in an immense output of women's academic and literary work. This generation of feminism has apparently entered a stage where we find the phenomena of femocrats, equal rights fights, lesbians seeking visibility (that is, acceptance in the straight world), genre writing and new age spiritualism which is again squeezing women back into frames. Little boxes.

The genre is indeed enjoying great popularity. To gain the acceptance which is necessary for this, the central core of the formula must be fundamentally male—even though it is written by women. Women's complete autonomy or deep complex friendships with each other are not issues, are blatantly left out of the plots. In *Still Murder*, I framed the central female character several times. Both beginning and end voices are male. The detective, Margot, whose narrative precedes and follows that of Patricia, is heterosexual. To put my real concerns into publishable form, I had to call my central character mad. Quite plainly I am playing with the suspense and pace of the detective fiction genre. And for me, the Margot parts of the book were the most boring to rewrite. She is like a femocrat who wants reform within the system, is paid to write policy for departments of the Status of Women, and as they in their pamphlets assiduously avoid mentioning 'lesbian', Margot is frightened of being called one. Similarly they have their genre writers.[5] If women can't love women, and I don't mean fuck with them, what is feminism?

Death *par excellence* seems to have entered the male millennial mind. Even the subtleties of television's Colombo have lost favour with the contemporary consumer of fiction, be it in video or book.

So the sheer femininity of the women genre writers feels clean. It's interesting that the mass murderers of late have killed mainly women, and that the judges will allow the excuse that his mother treated him badly. I often wonder how a mother can treat a male child *that* badly, yet in all the reporting it is proposed as an explanation. What on earth can she have done? She can never have nightly raped him as happens to far too many girl children: girls who live in terror of the footstep in the hall, the shadow across the night-light, their mothers told 'I'm just going to the loo, dear', rarely grow up to murder many, and if they did, the mind-numbing incest is never an excuse.

Psycho man is taking up the fictional air—by that I mean venues for the entertainment of escape. There are so many explorations and rationalisations of it. So much games-playing around it. The same story: kill cleverly. Win. Video games in parlours, in the home, and in truly *fin-de-siècle* style, bring in wizards and wizardry. Yet again, try to co-opt a female art, magic. But never the woman's story. It is no good ignoring what is happening around women today, so the boy in *Still Murder* is a suggestion of that outside world. He is not a full-blown character because women do try and stay away from that style of entertainment. They don't understand it. You hardly see a female face in those games parlours.

Dale Spender in a recent newspaper article suggested that women are in print more now because men are more interested in control of the computer and the video. For all the sales of feminine genre novels, few have been transformed into the audiovisual media, which has the large market share of escape fiction. Still, women must read.

Death—murder—is essential in whodunits. Who stole the necklace doesn't grab the modern mind any more. If there's murder, there's a killer. Motives in the genre are generally pretty shallow and not women's things at all. Women commit less than 1 per cent of murders in the world, or .01 per cent, I can't remember. So my woman murders, but her murder is surrounded by meditations on war. Her .01 body is lost in the thousands, but why she did it is the intrigue.

It's a matter of seriousness. Killing is a part of the male psyche and war characterises the millennia of patriarchal states. Male genre writers can proselytise their politics both in dialogue and plot sequence because killing for the reasons of power, sexual jealousy and money—the usual motives—make sense. Women cannot be so blatant because our concerns are marginalised in the fabric of the culture. If the culture is to be believed women are acted upon not active, painted not painting. If my females were to be active, in the full fictional sense of the word, they would have to be the murderer and the detective. I brought the margin into the frame and the frame into the text.

I have a book[6] with 220 illustrations of the work done by women artists in the time parallel to the golden age of detective fiction, the 1920s, 1930s and the war, then the 1950s. Radical changes in fashions occurred during this time, too, starting with the boyish look for women. The genre, the framed painting and photograph, the fashion, are all designated, fenced-off areas, where a woman might achieve freedom of expression. Like libertarian movements in sexual practices, these appear to give women more freedom, but in essence they don't. Within that confined space, she may express bravery or bravado, intelligence or cleverness, personal liberty or exposition of entrapment, but it's all the same to the world. They needn't take it seriously, because it is within a frame. It isn't, thus specified, truly challenging. Even so, efforts have been made to suppress their work of the women associated with the surrealist movement, to forget their names, to undervalue what they did, to take them out of the art histories, though the work was no less accomplished. While Andre Breton wrote the theory of the *enfant femme* as the muse, the women there respond: to you I am a Muse, well here I am, painting myself, this is your Muse. And my (her, our) Muse? In such an illustration, how can anyone believe in role reversal?

It is amazing how many self-portraits the women painters painted.

Women must read. Well imagine, you're at home, the kids want this, the blokes want that, how much of the house's VCR is the woman going to control? She resorts to her romance fiction, her adventure fiction, her rich-bitch fiction or the new mystery books by young women. She reads the terribly sophisticated talk of an academic who happens to be a detective on the side. She reads about the impossible: that a woman is head of Homicide in New South Wales and gets her offsider to do the legwork for her while she struggles with her relationship, and she appreciates being taken down the Spit Road in a fast car and recognising parts of Sydney. She reads about a gutsy young woman in Chicago taking on the power-brokers. She has a secret life in a box, a life where good triumphs. All these books in the local library have marks which show how well read the new mystery genre is.

Many feminist lesbians have a wide library of the new woman detective novels. They love them. They too want to escape and are really glad that women are up and published. Having read all of Margery Allingham and Dorothy Sayers and Agatha Christie et al, she relates it in some degree to her own lifestyle, and enjoys it as a cricket lover can sit through the five days of a Test match.

So is the genre a space away from the reigning hostile reality, or is it a frame showing the 'vulgar'[7] lives of the other half? Women's little kitchen cubes, where money means vegetables and intelligence is necessary if food is to be put on the table without embarrassment or nervous strain, are where logic and commonsense rule. Feminists have widened that particular cube. Nevertheless, the outer reality is controlled by an alien consciousness. Intellectual women never take these genre writers seriously and admit to reading them rather defiantly. They are indeed getting a minor thrill from them, because somewhere there with all the role-reversal fiats, give talk is going on. Friendship in the fictional sphere. They know they're not serious, for really how many murders does your average village spinster come across?

The great women formula writers accepted the rules. And bent them in a different way from their male counterparts. While the men introduced 1930s socialism, the women became more intrigued with the puzzle, the working out of clues, etc. Did they curb their literary talents to fit so they could be published, or did they just want to write like that? Who bothers with the names? Josephine Tey? Pamela Branch? Lucy Malleson, whose pseudonyms were Anthony Gilbert and Marion Mainwaring? One might go to the library for some holiday reading and pick up one of these novels or one of the new ones. They're interchangeable as entertainment, though some might disappoint, some might bore and some entrance. It is the nature of that kind of reading that you do judge a book by its cover, and take pot luck. The quality of the work is within its frame.

When I decided to play with the genre, it mattered to me whether a woman had ever been appointed to the New South Wales Homicide squad, and I found out that none had. I suspect it may have mattered to Dorothy Sayers—the way she loves to go into technical detail about facts. The point is the facts you put into a fiction reflect your opinion. Especially in genre where the moral of the tale supports both writer's and reader's sense of self-virtue. One must be aware of what philosophy of life one is propagating. If one's grand leap into make-believe was role reversal, or assuming for a woman a job jealously guarded by men, thus accepting reality and showing it as it is, then one is propagating a predominantly male view of the world, no matter how impossible to believe you are in it.

I wanted to be believed and the genre became a sounding board to bounce ideas off. A body; a number of suspects; a detective who has a problem to solve and gets beaten up along the track; the string of suspense; whodunit and how. Teasing the genre became part of the literary interest. For whether the readers were women in their kitchen cubes or lesbian feminist academics, they, drawing from their genre reading and from real life, could understand. Constant literary experiment is reflective of action in the women's movement, suggesting the question: how can we influence history and culture?

As everyone is political, some women writers seem to be making deliberately conservative, reformist choices in what and how they write. Equal rights fights certainly aren't won, and if they were, they are men's rights. You'd become a cock in a frock, as a friend of mine would say. I want to find women's rights, and the formula of genre writing simply won't allow it, for how many women seriously consider murdering someone? And for money? For power? I prefer the truth of the peasants, not the pomposity of bourgeoisie, be shown in the frames. Idealistic as it may sound, unpopular as it appears to be, and dangerous as it might prove to be to my continuing success, I take Virginia Woolf's questions to heart. I am interested in influencing history and culture. The female reality to me is the truth, and the violence intrinsic to the structure of whodunits is not a common feminine characteristic, though it is predominant in the society. Because we have not been able to build on women's thought, from the time, say, of Christine de Pizan in the fourteenth century,[8] each generation of thinking women has to work it out for itself, and the load is so great, even if we had the room and someone else doing our washing and cooking, we get worn out going over the same wide ground. I have to accept the frames society or the culture allows me, otherwise I am unheard. The popularity of the genre was there; I merely had to use it, tease it, be funny with it, and leave the interpretation of the truths up to the readers. The various voices in *Still Murder* are doors through which different readers can come into my fiction, and one of those doors is a female detective.

NOTES

1. John Berger, *Ways of Seeing*, BBC, 1972, p. 103. 'The so-called "genre" picture—the picture of "low life"—was thought of as the opposite of the mythological picture. It was vulgar instead of noble. The purpose of the "genre" picture was to prove—either positively or negatively—that virtue in this world was rewarded by social and financial success. Thus, those who could afford to buy these pictures—cheap as they were—had their own virtue confirmed. Such pictures were particularly popular with the newly arrived bourgeoisie who identified themselves not with the characters painted but with the moral which the scene illustrated.'

2. Dale Spender has brought out a book by this title, Pandora Press, London, 1983.

3. Both Amanda Cross and P.D. James show an alarming cynicism on the subject of women and general feminist tenets. While Barbara Wilson attempts some kind of political awareness in that she deals with refuges, collectives, prostitution, rape, etc., Sarah Dreher, Katherine V. Forrest and Claire McNab seem chiefly concerned with their own sexuality, begging for its entrance into the mainstream, not seeing lesbianism as a political rejection of heteropatriarchy (which it is whether they like it or not).

4. Maureen Hill, *Women of the Twentieth Century*, Chapmans, London, 1991.

5. Writers like Antonia Fraser, Jennifer Rowe, Sarah Caudwall, Sara Paretsky, show women acting within spheres of influence, with jobs, with success, who never approach women's issues.

6. Whitney Chadwick, *Women Artists and the Surrealist Movement*, Thames & Hudson, 1985.

7. Berger, p. 104. '[In Hals' paintings of fisherboys] they smile at the better-off—to ingratiate themselves, but also at the prospect of a sale or a job.' Obversely, the woman reader smiles at the better off, in that the fictional heroines are either rich or live in a world in which logic prevails.

8. Christine de Pizan, *The Book of the City of Ladies*, Picador, 1983, pp. 160-1. '11.44.1 . . . I am therefore troubled and grieved when men argue that many women want to be raped and that it does not bother them at all to be raped by men even when they verbally protest. It would be hard to believe such villainy is actually pleasant for them.'

The front pages describe de Pizan's significance: 'From 1930 on, Christine (sic) wrote more than twenty distinguished works, nearly all concerned with two themes: the political life of France and the defence of womankind.'

SUSAN GEASON

Susan Geason was born in Tasmania, raised in Brisbane, lived and studied in Canada for some years and is now a denizen of inner-city Sydney. With an MA in political philosophy, she has been a policy adviser to federal and state governments, a journalist and a freelancer specialising in criminology, the environment and writing for governments. Shaved Fish, *her book of short stories and* Dogfish, *a novel featuring PI Syd Fish, are now in their second printing. In the mid-sixties Geason was one of the five women on the University of Queensland's student council and was the first woman to wear trousers on campus. She got her first taste of journalism—and the male backlash—writing a feminist column for the student newspaper. In 1972, while studying at the University of Toronto, she ran the first Ontario Conference on Women, featuring most of that province's female movers and shakers.*

Ain't Misbehavin'

SUSAN GEASON

> *Girls should be allowed to play in the mud. They should be released from the obligations of perfection. Some of your writing, at least, should be as evanescent as play.* Margaret Atwood, 'Nine Beginnings', in *The Writer on Her Work* ((ed.) Janet Sternburg, Virago, 1992).

This essay argues that those writers who have tried to combine feminism with the private eye genre have too often sacrificed art to ideology, have placed impossible pressures on character and plot in pursuit of ideological purity. By creating heroines who are too good to be true, they have often undermined their characters' credibility.

These feminist PIs are moral absolutists when many of the male PIs are more believable moral relativists.

I put this down to a number of factors: first, these heroines are the direct descendants of morally uplifting literature for girls (Little Eva, various dying swans from Dickens, the March women, Katy Carr, the virgin martyrs, Jane Eyre, etc—not to mention all the female masochism we later osmosed from Charlotte Bronte, Jean Rhys, Rosamond Lehmann, Georgette Heyer and their ilk); secondly, they have been influenced by the Puritan wing of the American feminist movement which largely sees the female role as one of service to a higher good; thirdly, they have been influenced by 1960s left-liberalism; and finally, the example of Raymond Chandler's Philip Marlowe legitimised the private eye as moral crusader and social outsider.

I try to show, too, that Australian feminist private eye writers are less ideology driven than their American counterparts.

I also contend that this political correctness appears to be breaking down. Feminist PIs are becoming less morally absolute, less marginalised, are acting more like real women and less like feminist exemplars, and are becoming much richer, more complex characters. This I see as a change for the better, as it is likely to attract a wider audience for a sub-genre which has too often preached to the converted.

Finally, I show how Syd Fish fits into this schema and articulate my own agenda as a female PI writer.

FEMINIST PIS: TOO GOOD TO BE TRUE?

Too many female detectives remind me of Jo March with a blackbelt. They're just too good to be true. To employ a cinema metaphor, they're June Allyson playing Barbara Stanwyck roles. Maybe feminists have created women who are coldly perfect and perfectly cold.

The problem is that perfect characters make for a boring read (and a boring write). They are inflexible and predictable. Let's face it, enormous skill is required to make the virtuous interesting (remember the Lives of the Saints?); the only great good women who come easily to mind are Jane Eyre and Dorothea Casaubon, but that's the big league.

Let's look at some feminist PIs. V.I. Warshawski, Sara Paretsky's immensely successful creation, leads an empty life. Until recently she didn't take lovers and her closest friends were much older parent substitutes—Dr Lotty Herschel and Salvatore

Contreras. Vic drove an old car and didn't spend any money on herself.

Sue Grafton's Kinsey Millhone seems oddly marginal, too. Until recently, she lived in a garage and had an octogenarian male as her best friend (there are lots of surrogate fathers in feminist PI books, but no mothers of any kind in the male variety—worth a closer look by scholars of the genre.) Totally devoid of personal vanity and consumerism, Kinsey jogs and lifts weights, cuts her own hair and drives an ancient Volkswagen. She does, thank God, have the occasional fling with a man.

Barbara Wilson's Pam Nilsen is lesbian, left wing, vegetarian and working in a print collective that doesn't take any ideologically unsound jobs. Her only discernible fault is jealousy of her twin sister. Maureen Moore's Marsha Lewis appears to have been assembled from a left-liberal, feminist kit. Living with a surrogate aunt, she studies for an MA in urban anthropology, mashes vegetables for her little girl and bakes bread, drives a bomb and boycotts politically suspect products in supermarkets. In grimy, gloomy England, Liza Cody's Anna Lee was driven to adopting Selwyn and Bea, the odious couple downstairs, as a surrogate family.

Not one of these has a problem with drugs or alcohol or is sexually promiscuous (in this they remind me irresistibly of Mary Higgins Clarke's pert, plucky, semi-liberated heroines, which would horrify most of their creators). When they do get it on, it's behind the arras.

THE SEDUCTION OF BEING GOOD

Why have feminist PI writers fallen into the trap of creating good girls? A mixture of conditioning, ideology and lack of confidence are the reasons, I suspect, and because they're so busy being good girls themselves. American writer Mary Gordon hit upon a profound female truth when she wrote that, 'There is no seduction like that of being thought a good girl.'

Most of us were force fed *Rebecca of Sunnybrook Farm*, *Anne of Green Gables*, *Pollyanna*, the March women, and Katy Carr and Clover at an impressionable age, and that sort of conditioning is difficult to overcome.

Another reason for creating female PIs who don't cheat or screw around or occasionally act irresponsibly is that feminists didn't want to hand the enemy ammunition. We see this principle operating with minority groups who block any revelations about the group which could bring bad publicity. One example of this was African-Americans' outrage at Anita Hill's washing of dirty linen in public when she charged a US Supreme Court nominee, Clarence Thomas, with sexual harassment; another is the silence that for too long has surrounded Aboriginal men's violence towards Aboriginal women. All this is self-censorship, and though it's understandable, it's to be deplored, because it simply exchanges one straitjacket for another. It's also the enemy of truth and totalitarian in tendency.

So while women writers have dared put tough female PIs on the street, until recently they've been pulling their punches. Female PIs have been turned into role models, exemplars, not people, facing the same demands as women in other male bastions—to be twice as smart, twice as hard-working and totally irreproachable.

And just as these expectations hobble women in the boardroom, they handicap female private investigators. It's the *Schoolgirls' Own* mentality, where you send in spunky virgins to fight the demon Hun with only a good British sense of right and wrong, a nailfile and their own wits to assist them. (This type of sleuth actually has a long tradition in private eye fiction.)

I'm not saying our heroines should be as morally slippery as Sam Spade, but at least there should be some sense of struggle and the occasional temptation left unresisted.

AIN'T MISBEHAVIN'

THE FREEDOM TO BE BAD

At the risk of sounding like a conspiracy theorist, I see the hand of
the American Puritan wing of the feminist movement in all this.
Left-liberal politically, this school of thought holds that liberation
doesn't mean the freedom to choose to be as rotten as men, but
rather the freedom to be more virtuous and ideologically sound.
This means women can be legal aid lawyers or social workers but
not stockbrokers or tycoons, and that women who beat men on their
own terms, like Margaret Thatcher, are disowned. Some people—
including me—do not think this is what is meant by freedom.

Translated into the crime genre, it means that female PIs will
be social workers in disguise, won't carry guns and won't take jobs
from crooks. Even lawyers don't have such impossible standards
or affect such moral omnipotence. By definition, criminal lawyers
work mostly for people who have broken the law, and as long as
clients charged with murder don't confess, lawyers proceed on the
assumption that they are innocent till proven guilty and that they
deserve the best defence available.

To get away with this absolutist moral position, feminist PIs
have to be outsiders—marginals.

PHILIP MARLOWE IN DRAG

Raymond Chandler made all this possible. Our heroines are the
spiritual successors of Philip Marlowe; perennial outsiders who
don't seem to need family, friends or sex, meaning they don't have
to compromise like ordinary folk.

It was with the stories and novels of Chandler and Dashiell
Hammett that the private eye entered the literary mainstream. A
mass readership was already addicted to the hard-boiled, violent
escapades of PIs in pulp magazines such as *Black Mask*, but the
street-cred of Hammett's Sam Spade and the romanticism of

Chandler's Philip Marlowe—and the stylish writing of both—revolutionised the image of the PI and attracted a more discriminating audience.

Hammett and Chandler have become the twin pillars of the hard-boiled PI tradition. Insofar as the genre can ever be realistic, Hammett's work is on the realistic end of the continuum, while Chandler's is on the romantic. The reasons are plain: Hammett drew upon years of experience as a Pinkerton agent, whereas Chandler got all his information about the underworld second hand. Much of it came straight from his imagination.

Sam Spade is thus closer to the real-life PIs we know and love from Royal Commissions and anti-corruption inquiries. Hammett's hero regards bribing or blackmailing public officials for information as normal business practice, takes bribes himself on occasions, commits adultery with his partner's wife and has an affair with a major murder suspect. He is a moral relativist.

Chandler's Philip Marlowe, on the other hand, is a moral absolutist. He regards himself as a moral crusader, and is incorruptible and alarmingly chaste.

It is virtually impossible for anyone practising in the genre now to avoid the influence of one or both of these giants. The sons of Hammett include James Crumley's Milo Milodragovich and C.W. Sughrue, James Lee Burke's Dave Robicheaux, Gerald Petrievich's anti-heroes, Jonathan Latimer's Bill Crane, Lawrence Block's Matt Scudder, Robert Crais's Elvis Cole, Robert Barrett's Les Norton (who probably owes more to Mickey Spillane, in fact), Dan Kavanagh's Duffy, Loren D. Estleman's Amos Walker and all the characters created by Elmore Leonard, Charles Willeford, and James Ellroy.

Chandler's children include Ross Macdonald's Lew Archer, Robert Parker's Spenser, Earl R. Emerson's Thomas Black, Peter Corris's Cliff Hardy, Robert Campbell's Jimmy Flannery, Bill Pronzini's nameless detective, Michael Lewin's Albert Samson and all the feminist PIs.

You could say that the feminist PIs are Philip Marlowe in drag.

HAMMETT'S BOYS

Unlike their female counterparts, many of the male PIs are deeply flawed characters, and it's their defects and conflicts that make them interesting. Scudder spends most of one novel in Alcoholics Anonymous meetings, and other famous alcoholic PIs include Milo Milodragovich, C.W. Sughrue, Dave Robicheaux and Bill Crane. Nick and Nora Charles drank too much (as did their creator), and of course Sherlock Holmes was a snowbird (a term for a cocaine addict I think I read in a 1930s novel). You even meet the occasional American male PI who's a substance abuser.

Many male PIs are also addicted to violence. That's why they're PIs: it's a licence to consort with crims and beat up baddies, all in the name of justice (the law doesn't tend to come into it). Dave Robicheaux, for example, often takes the law into his own hands and anguishes over his attraction to violence; Milo Milodragovich is self-destructive and dangerous when drunk; Duffy is voraciously bisexual and, as an ex-cop, regards the law as an ass; Les Norton is a violent, sexist yob, and even Spenser resorts to using an African-American sidekick armed with heavy artillery to settle scores for him.

For all their posturing, female PIs must have a similar attraction to the seamy side (the same holds true for all sorts of do-gooders, surely) otherwise they'd be physiotherapists or lecture in semiotics, but that fascination with evil is never made explicit in feminist crime: is it something they're not prepared to admit? Are they ashamed of it? Why can't they just get down and boogie? Why do they have to overcompensate by acting like Mother Superior on a *pro-bono* case for the Holy Spirit?

THE AUSTRALIAN VARIANT

While the influence of both Raymond Chandler and the American feminists on Australian female PIs is obvious, they are not simple clones; in fact they exhibit a decidedly Australian point of view.

Perhaps because of some deep-rooted suspicion of ideology for its own sake in the Australian psyche, our feminist writers are less politically correct and more morally and ethically flexible than their American or British counterparts, who sometimes sound like secular nuns.

Marele Day's Claudia Valentine, for example, has done the unthinkable and walked out on her children, who are being raised by a stepmother. Inspector Carole Ashton—Claire McNab's lesbian protagonist—raced off a prime suspect in one of her cases and moved her in, and let a former lover cloud her judgment in another novel. McNab's sex scenes are unusually steamy for female crime writing. Ashton is now threatening to leave the police force and come out as a lesbian PI.

Phryne Fisher, Kerry Greenwood's flapper detective, is an unashamed vamp who has trouble keeping her silk knickers on. Even Jennifer Rowe's Verity Birdwood is a defiantly unsympathetic character.

From the start, Australian feminists reserved the right to drink in pubs and dance on tables as well as marching for abortion on demand. Our feminist PI writers are jealously guarding this hard-won right to have fun and still be taken seriously.

BOREDOM BACKLASH

This Australian suspicion of political correctness is not only artistically sound, it's also good business: one-dimensional characters can wear thin, as the bad reviews for a recent Sue Grafton effort demonstrated. And if the fans are getting a bit jaded, the critics are becoming downright scathing. Here is the influential Marilyn Stasio (*New York Times Book Review*, 5 January 1992) talking about Linda Grant's latest Catherine Sayler mystery:

> *But how they do quack, these characters who line up like docile ducks in their too-good-to-be-true ranks. Catherine herself always speaks ex cathedra, delivering ideologically unimpeachable position-lectures on every social malady from murder to junk-food addiction. 'I think of myself as an open-minded person,' she says, 'tolerant of others' ways.' Don't believe it for a minute.*

Who hasn't voiced a similar complaint at some time?

SIGNS OF CHANGE

The good news is that it's starting to look as if we were only going through a phase, a period of transition. Change is coming. Maybe it's just the 1990s—mid-life crisis time for baby boomers worldwide—but maybe it's also due to a growing confidence, a realisation that we can let our girl guides grow up and act sexy and have some doubts.

Sue Grafton got the message and provided Kinsey Millhone with a new apartment, a man, and a hairdresser. Maybe she'll even go out and buy some clothes. Across the Atlantic, Anna Lee fled drizzly London and her dismal colleagues for Florida, got mixed up in all sorts of American mayhem, and had a torrid fling with a sexy Yank. At the same time, her landlord sold the building, casting her out of the nest, and her odious neighbours split up and moved away.

The American adventure also seems to have galvanised Cody into ditching Anna in favour of a much more aggressive PI, Eva

Wylie, 'big, ugly and irresistible, a female wrestler with criminal tendencies and large pectorals', according to the publicity. Apparently when Eva is not working the sleazy wrestling circuit, she's a security guard living in a wrecker's yard with two dogs.

Now that's progress.

Back in Chicago, Vic Warshawski, pushing forty, is busting out all over, buying a sporty, gas-guzzling Trans Am sports car, bedding an African-American cop and gaining some insights into her inability to commit. Sandra Scoppettone, who wrote police procedurals as Jack Early, has come out with lesbian detective Lauren Laurano, who won't give up junk food despite escalating cholesterol levels, and who became so obsessed with computers in one adventure that she neglected her psychiatrist lover and caused fights.

Perhaps Verity Birdwood will surprise us all and take a lover.

SYDNEY FISH, PRIVATE EYE

There was no conscious decision to make my private eye male. I'd been writing 'literary', non-comic short stories with female protagonists, but Syd touched down fully developed. As a sleazy press secretary, he just had to be male: it's the nature of the beast.

I wasn't reading much detective fiction at the time, so my influences were probably old ones—Chandler, Hammett, Macdonald, and Damon Runyon.

By the second story it became obvious to me that Syd needed a civilising influence, and Lizzie Darcy was born. I soon recognised Lizzie's potential as a change agent, not only for Syd, but for male readers (and besides she's partly me, bullying all the men I ever knew).

So while Syd could never be called a feminist, there is a feminist agenda in the stories. Oddly enough, what critic Stephen Knight called the subterranean feminism in the Fish books eluded not only many male readers, but also the odd member of the female ideological police—one woman reviewer even calling Syd 'vulgar, sexist and homophobic'. (Appalled, I checked with a gay bookshop in Sydney's Oxford Street and discovered they were recommending *Dogfish*.)

Syd falls squarely into the morally relative camp. For a start he's an inner city, formerly working-class lad who grew up with a healthy disrespect for the law, cant, pomposity and spurious class distinctions. He comes to the job of private investigator via the yellow press and politics, both areas demanding moral flexibility and a strong stomach.

Recognising that you can't make omelettes without cracking eggs, Syd is not above breaking into houses, lying, changing sides and calling on Luther Huck when he needs muscle, recognising that he's not tough enough to frighten the sorts of low lifes he confronts in his business without a gun. (As it was my hatred of guns that handicapped Syd, I compensated by inventing Luther Huck, who wouldn't know a moral from a Mauser.) Now if I won't pit Syd—a semi-tough bloke—against the Sydney milieu, I certainly wouldn't send in an unarmed woman and (a) expect her to survive and (b) expect my readers to believe it.

I've also refused to make Syd a marginal. He's solidly grounded in the eastern suburbs where he grew up, knows lots of people, has networks he can use, has racked up favours he can call in, and knows exactly how Sydney works. He makes friends with people he meets through his work, is highly dependent on Lizzie Darcy and has fallen hopelessly in love with Julia Western. He gets on well with losers and low lifes and 'is no stranger to sleaze'.

Syd is politically incorrect on a number of grounds, too. He eats the wrong food (pizzas, takeout Mexican, too much beer), stages male tantrums (about Julia's career aspirations, about Lizzie's love affairs), leches after women (the female police officer, the pornographer's wife, Lucy), refuses to jog, persecutes fools (the merchant banker, the town planner), exhibits poor judgment about character (Andrew 'the Greek' Kotsopoulos, Fiona McLeod) and has to be pulled up regularly by Lizzie for his sexist attitudes.

But all this makes him 'real', I believe. As real as any fictional PI can be, anyway.

SELLING THE MESSAGE

Some female writers seem to have created feminist PIs to make a point about women's capabilities in traditionally male fields of endeavour. Has it worked?

While I don't have any statistics on the female–male breakdown in readership of Paretsky and Grafton, I suspect the bulk of their readers are female. It's fine to be a role model for girls (though I wouldn't advise any of them to try their self-defence class karate against a couple of football players), but is this enough? If I sometimes find them puritanical, humourless, one-dimensional, sexless drudges, it's highly probable that they aren't reaching the sort of audience that needs its pills sugar coated—most men, for example.

If men read my books, and they seem to, it's probably because the humour and the recognition factor mask the message. I'm endeavouring to persuade and teach by example, not coerce or preach to the converted. A typical Aussie male in the process of a sometimes painful, sometimes rewarding transition, Syd is being forced to take women seriously. Why? Because they can match or better him on every test except physical strength, because they are loyal and tolerant, and because he can talk to them.

I'm optimistic enough to hope that when Syd learns some lesson about his relationship to women and the world, the male readers will learn something too. The fact that Syd is far from perfect, that he's growing and learning in each outing, prevents him from becoming a formulistic chore for me, and I hope makes him more interesting to readers.

Trying to see the world through male eyes is a technical challenge, and so far nobody has accused him of sounding like a woman (though my friends often say they can hear me talking). It tests my observational skills, my grasp of male psychology and most of all my empathy. And it's fun for me to look at female characters through men's eyes.

Despite my criticisms, I am heartened by the signs of change in the genre. I firmly believe that complex, flawed characters are more appealing to readers than impossibly perfect, impossibly strong, totally alienated women who don't seem to be able to do two things at a time. Why can't Kinsey Millhone show her legs occasionally? Why can't Vic Warshawski have a decent social life? Why doesn't Anna Lee get the hell out of that awful detective agency and set up by herself? Why can't they ever go to the pub and get pissed and dance on the table? Where's their sense of humour?

Maybe that's coming.

MARELE DAY

Marele Day is a Sydney-based writer whose work experience ranges from fruit picking to academic teaching. She is a lecturer and editor and was writer in residence at the University of Wollongong, NSW in 1992. Her poems, stories and literary criticism have appeared in numerous newspapers and magazines and she has been the recipient of three Australia Council grants. She is best known for her thrillers featuring Australia's first female private eye, Claudia Valentine—The Life and Crimes of Harry Lavender, The Case of the Chinese Boxes *and* The Last Tango of Delores Delgado, *which has been nominated for the Shamus Awards, 1993.*

'Bitch City'

MARELE DAY

The Kid and the Man from Pinkertons

*It was early morning. The man from Pinkertons headed west.
He looked odd out here driving along in a trench coat and a
city hat but that didn't worry him none. He knew how to track
his man, the city was the same kind of wilderness as the west. A
wasteland full of the same kind of desperadoes, same corrupt
cattle barons, same sheriffs working for them.*

*He stopped. There were hoof marks leading away from the
remains of a campfire. He got out of the car. The Kid couldn't
be too far ahead judging by the still warm embers. The man
from Pinkertons raised the binoculars to his eyes. A flurry of
dust up ahead. It had to be the Kid. Nineteen years old and
he'd killed thirty-seven men already. There was a price on his
head as big as Texas. Not that the man from Pinkertons was
thinking about that. He had a job to do, was all.*

*He got back in the car, adjusted the tilt of his hat and thought
of the motto he worked by—'the eye that never sleeps'. He
fingered the sleek metal shaft of the gun in his pocket and smiled
to himself. By the end of the day one of them would be dead.
The man from Pinkertons didn't aim for it to be him.*

The hard-boiled American-style detective story has a lot in common with the western—it is an adventure story rather than a puzzle to be solved, and there is plenty of action often erupting in violence. The hero knows his way around the traps yet distrusts society and has his own personal code of ethics, a grey knight in a black world. He knows his way around the traps because he knows the place; this is the landscape of his quest, his scene of action. Man against man, man against his environment. A machismo paradise, not a good woman in sight.

These stories also share a strong sense of place, a focus on 'where' the action occurs. Central to the western as a genre is the focus on the scene of the action. The western signifies more than the area of the United States west of the Mississippi; it also has a symbolic dimension. The 'home' of the gunfighter is the west, the wilderness where no woman could follow. Towns and cities were civilisation and women a civilising influence. The gunfighter did his best to stay away from them. As long as he stayed out of town, away from the church women trying to tame him and get him to the altar, or the bar girls at the other end of town enticing him with the pleasures of the flesh, he was safe; his masculine strength remained intact. But soon the west was covered in cities and there was nowhere else the gunfighter could go. He donned a trench coat, kept the gun, swapped his horse for a car, his stetson for a fedora, and did his best not to become polluted by those mean streets.

It's not surprising then that the scene of action of the golden age writers of detective fiction, Hammett and Chandler, were cities of the west—Los Angeles and San Francisco. Probably no accident also that Hollywood, the site where dream cities were built, that again and again and again recreated the symbolic landscape, was here too.

The place in hard-boiled detective fiction is an intersection of reality and fiction. It's a real city that becomes the site on which fictional cities are built, as well as a dais which may debate conflicting responses to social change. While English clue-puzzle detective fiction essentially has a Newtonian world view—established in an ordered universe in which everything is ultimately explainable, in which identification of the aberrant individual whodunit restores that order—the hard-boiled genre is very much more an Einsteinian world view; chaotic, variable, shifting.

Though *The Kid and the Man from Pinkertons* is a fabrication, Pinkertons Detective Agency did have operatives out hunting outlaws. Men from Pinkertons followed Butch Cassidy and the Sundance Kid into South America when they got so well known in the west they had to move on. They tracked Frank James and the McCoys. In history what got the outlaws in the end was the twentieth century. Posses could be rounded up by telephone, it wasn't one man pitted against another but one man pitted against a network. The twentieth century brought with it the New Woman, already heralded in the nineteenth. Pinkertons had always employed female operatives, starting in 1856 with Mrs Kate Warne who stayed with them till her death. She could 'worm out secrets in many places to which it was impossible for a male detective to gain access'.[1] There were even a few fictional adventuresses in the hard-boiled school such as Gale Gallagher (written by male novelist Will Oursler) but, curiously, their names don't spring as readily to mind as male toughs like Philip Marlowe, Sam Spade or Mike Hammer.

In 1900 journalist Bernard Owen observed that 'almost every profession has now opened its doors to women . . . the days when the single woman had no prospect but to do domestic service, needlework, or teaching as a means of keeping body and soul together have gone . . . it is not unlikely that the twentieth century will develop into a kind of golden age for women.'[2] Ninety years later this optimism is almost quaint, but there is no doubt that the increasing involvement of women in public life was really beginning to worry some people.

The decade of the 1920s which gave women the vote was also

the decade that gave rise to hard-boiled detective fiction. If women could no longer be contained at home, if they insisted on grabbing a piece of the action in the big world, something had to be done about it. As Anne Cranny-Francis comments: 'The hard-boiled detective represents a fictional resolution of the challenge to patriarchy posed by the twentieth-century Women's Movement.'³

If you couldn't keep them out of the city in the real world (and there were violent ways of doing that too) you could make sure the threat of them was diffused in the fictional city. How do you put Pandora back in her box, shut the woman up in the house again? The city metaphor attempts to provide two ways of doing this. First you make the streets so mean and tough that no (self-respecting) woman would ever want to venture out, and second you start calling the woman who does venture out names, show the treachery inherent in this new power unleashed in the city.

In the novels of Chandler, Hammett and particularly Spillane, women are depicted as victims or villains, more often villains. They come to you for help and they end up betraying you. Like the knights of old, you start off fighting dragons for them, to find in the end they weren't worth rescuing. The hero wants it to be a man's world, wants the streets to be so mean and tough that no woman would ever dare walk them, so labyrinthine that only the hero knows his way around, yet the threat of the feminine is ever present.

> The bitch city is something different on Saturday night, sophisticated in black, scented and powdered, but somehow not as unassailable, shiveringly beautiful in a haze of blinking lights. Reds and oranges, electric blues and vibrant greens assault the eye incessantly, and the resultant turn-on is as sweet as a quick sharp fix in a penthouse pad, a liquid cool that conjures dreams of towering glass spires and enameled minarets. There is excitement in this city on Saturday night, but it is tempered by

romantic expectancy. She is not a bitch, this city. Not on
Saturday night.[4]

In Ed McBain's world the city is a bitch, beautiful and corrupt. But powerful. The hard-boiled dick is continually trying to find a way around her without succumbing. She is like the women in the stories—seductive, dangerous and treacherous. What Ed McBain doesn't mention is that the place and the person don't start off corrupt, they become that way. On the virginal site men build the city of their dreams, but once built on, the site is no longer virginal, it is tainted with his touch. Somehow the dream develops a life on its own. And the virgin becomes a bitch.

How then does the female hard-boiled detective relate to this vision of city, negotiate her way around such a place? Is the city similarly threatening, or is there more than one story to be read there?

The depiction of city is of particular interest to me because my original motivation for writing Claudia Valentine thrillers was an interest in a place rather than a protagonist. I wanted to write a book in which Sydney was the 'character', living, breathing, which generated the human characters in the story. From that came the idea to work in the hard-boiled genre because in this genre, the city is not simply a backdrop but has a sense of presence.

So what is Claudia Valentine's city like? Is it a bitch too? On one level it has to be because that's the game I'm playing. You have to play the game to change the game.

As in Ed McBain's bitch city, Claudia Valentine's Sydney is evoked with images of corruption.

She'd been a very sickly child, poxy and plague-ridden. But
she'd grown strong, like a mushroom on a dung heap. Like an
exotic mushroom I'd seen once at Gary's. A beautiful crimson
fungus had sprung out of the ground like a spider flower. But in

its centre was a dark foetid substance that smelled exactly like human excrement.[5]

She's 'cute, flighty and ultimately dangerous', as unpredictable as the weather. She's a narcissist craning to see her image in the reflective glass of city buildings. Bitches are unpredictable, volatile. If you can't contain them how do you control them? They can switch on the charm and suck you in, then turn around and betray you. There's no telling what they might do, there's no guidelines, they don't follow any rules. Hard-boiled detective fiction isn't the only place where twentieth century city life appears as chaotic and unpredictable, but it does seem ideally suited to such a depiction. The labyrinthine plot reflects this chaos, this lack of any inherent order. The clue-puzzle mystery restores order by identifying the aberrant individual responsible for that body on page two; in the hard-boiled thriller the body on page two merely serves as an entry point to the labyrinthine plot. Webs of conspiracy and corruption—sometimes it's as if the whole city is responsible for the crime. And maybe that's the point.

When I started to write about the city I was most interested in the difference between surface and depth, between how things appeared to be and how they really were. But I began to suspect that perhaps I would never know how things 'really were', that the layers of the fictional city were like a series of Chinese boxes— open one and what you find is another box which contains a box which contains a box and so on till you get to the last one that has in it only empty space.

The beautiful face with the corrupt body is a familiar cliché but this isn't the only way the difference between surface and depth can be imagised.

'My city was the most beautiful harbour in the world, a childhood of open doors . . .' Somewhere beneath the man-made layers, the surface structures of big businessmen and developers like the fictional Harry Lavender, lies a silent, more organic city that Claudia Valentine has access to, which is remembered and recorded by her. At the end of *The Life and Crimes of Harry Lavender* this city literally opens up to her. The old Pyrmont Bridge, ironically now overlaid by that monument to private development, the monorail, opens up with Claudia safely on the other side of it and her pursuer falling through the gap into the murky waters of the harbour, to be swallowed up no doubt without a trace. This confirms the hard-boiled male detective's worst fear—the capacity of the bitch to engulf him, to swallow him up. But for Claudia, safely on the other side of the gap, it's a different story altogether.

This is a layer of the city that Claudia knows and loves, that she's grown up with, that was a kind of playmate till the big boys took over the game. There was garbage, but it wasn't seeping, pervading pollution. You could see what you were getting. There was crime, but somehow life was more neighbourly. You could at least tell the difference between the goodies and the baddies.

I can hear the strings of violins in this last paragraph but it's not simply a question of Claudia looking back in nostalgia. 'The governors have always tried to impose a shape on Sydney, a clean ordered mirror image.' The city that collaborates with Claudia is this older, more organic place, that in comparison with its overlay arose from the grass roots' level. The overlay, the surface, has been imposed from above by the men who run the city. To produce a place more ordered, more pleasing to the eye, they say. What Claudia's eye sees and what she tells is that in sanitising the place they are gutting it, removing its spiritedness. As a lobotomy might do. If the city refuses to comply, if she refuses to take lying down what they're doing to her for their own aggrandisement, there's only one thing left to do. Operate. Remove the organs of unwillingness.

But they never succeed completely. In *The Case of the Chinese Boxes* the now sanitised Dixon Street, a tourist attraction that used to be the 'heart' of Sydney's old Chinatown, is compared with the new Chinatown, Cabramatta (actually Vietnamese). In the sanitised Chinatown there are signs for tourists to follow so they don't get lost. The streets and the shops are laid out more clearly, the doors leading to secret gambling dens have (apparently) been closed. It is no longer the labyrinth. Cabramatta is a different story. The Australian dream suburb of square fibro and brick houses on blocks of land has been overlaid by a seeming labyrinth. All the signs are in Vietnamese, the shops make a 'colourful disordered display'. Disordered, Claudia remarks, to the eye not yet attuned to them. There are doors leading to gambling dens, invisible to the eye not attuned to them. The outsider might get lost in the labyrinth forever. Yet this part of the city is the expression of the people who live in it, they know their way around. When you know the place its shroud of mystery disappears.

The best way to get to know a place is to experience it first hand. In Claudia Valentine's city, sitting at home and being told about it is no substitute for getting in amongst it. This is perhaps the most significant change the entry of the female protagonist into the genre has brought. It is she who is out there having the adventure, she who is seeing it, she who is telling her story, she who is drawing new maps of the place. In her city you don't have to be that tough to walk the mean streets. Maybe that was all a con job to keep us at home.

But if the streets are new to you and they have a reputation for being tough, a little preparation may be required. Being prepared doesn't mean you have to go out in a male body, with a trench coat and a gun. Claudia Valentine arms herself with karate. She never goes looking for a fight, she likes to keep her brain intact. Given the chance she'll run, and doesn't think there's anything dishonourable in doing that.

The best way to feel comfortable on these streets is to map the place so you know your way around it. More importantly, mapmaking provides a way of claiming back those streets.

Mapping the city works on a number of levels. The city outside the book can be evoked by giving quite specific coordinate points. I've never been to Chicago but Paretsky's maps read like such careful and faithful representations that I could find my way around the real city by using her books. However, while there are points of resemblance, the city in her book is not exactly the same city as the one in Illinois. The mapmaker has added her own seraphs and cherubs, her own sea monsters, the creatures of her own imagination. She has also chosen which features of the landscape to include on the map. Though the cities that are the sites of action for feminist detective writers refer to real places, they also comment on the city as metaphorical landscape, as inherited from male writers, and read that differently as well as implanting new detail. Maybe for a woman the city's not such a bitch after all.

If the hard-boiled male detective comes to the story knowing the city like the back of his hand, the female detective shows how we might get to know it. Instead of staying silent, you do what all good detectives do—ask questions. One way men have kept women off their streets is to surround their 'domains' with an aura of impenetrability. Nowhere is this more evident than in heavy industry such as chemical plants and shipping, which are the loci of two of Paretsky's stories. The organisation of these technologies is tied to the plot and V.I. Warshawski must understand enough of the technology to allow her to solve the mystery. To solve/dissolve the mystery all it takes (as well as action) is a bit of observation and a few well-placed questions. Heavens above, technology can't be all that difficult if men know how to do it.

The city is bigger than the detective's beat and when Claudia Valentine goes beyond her range of known streets into unfamiliar terrain she is not afraid to ask directions or use a map. Men will drive around for hours rather than stop and ask someone for directions.

On another level the plot works as a map through the city, particularly if the structure of both is labyrinthine as has been suggested earlier. If the labyrinth is what we have to contend with the way not to get lost in it is to leave a thread. The murderer had left a thread, the clues the detective discovers is evidence of that thread. The detective follows that thread (usually backwards, moving from event to motivation) but lays over the back story (the what-really-happened) the thread of investigation and in turn the narrative thread, which tells the story of that investigation.

Traditionally, though a plot may have twists and turns, the telling of it had been pretty straightforward. This line that you get from joining the dots of clues and investigation, the dots of action and motivation, cause and effect, imposes a narrative ordering of the story. When all is chaos out there in the real world and even in the world depicted in the book, it is a great comfort to have this thread to show us the way. But comfort can make us complacent. We can be tricked into believing that this is the natural order of things. Feminist writing doesn't always follow this form. The straight line as the 'natural' shape of narrative can be questioned by disruption, fragmentation, multiplicity, circularity and other shapings. Though these may comment on the nature of the city, and while there may be the semblance of chaos, the narrative itself is not chaotic. There is someone carefully assembling the structure. The story doesn't just happen; someone has to be there to put the words on the page, to assess the alternatives.

Through the vehicle of the feminist detective the writer can record her impressions of the place as she adventures through it, get her voice heard, construct her city. Make it her own.

NOTES

1. Mrs Kate Warne, quoted in James D. Horan and Howard Swizzet, *The Pinkertons: The Dynasty That Made History*, Putnam, New York, 1951, p. 29.
2. Bernard Owen, quoted in *Crime on Her Mind*, (ed.) Michele B. Slung, Penguin, Ringwood, 1977, p. 20.
3. Anne Cranny-Francis, *Feminist Fiction*, Polity Press, Cambridge, 1990, p. 157.
4. Ed McBain, 'Fuzz', in *Detective Stories*, Octopus Books, London, 1984, p. 483.
5. Marele Day, *The Life and Crimes of Harry Lavender*, Allen & Unwin, Sydney, 1988, p. 47.

OTHER IMPRINT TITLES FROM ANGUS & ROBERTSON

Reading Tim Winton

I think the ordinary things of life are worthy of celebration.
They tend to be forgotten, particularly in this day and age . . .
In my stories I'm trying to render the commonplace worthy of attention.
And then to have it looked at anew.

TIM WINTON

R EADING TIM WINTON INCLUDES ESSAYS BY PROMINENT academics which cover the major aspects of Winton's work: his interest in place, the spiritual, childhood, history, and gender roles. It also includes a fascinating insight into Winton's own beliefs, especially about the practice of writing. This is the first full-length study of one of the most exciting voices in Australian fiction, an author whose wide appeal reflects the democratic strain in his writing.

Edited by Richard Rossiter and Lyn Jacobs

Only Lawyers Dancing

by Jan McKemmish

There it was. The threat. I knew it would come, but hard eyes and cruel mouths don't come upon a voice tape. I reach for his file and we go through the details until the phone rings for the next appointment. It is only 9.00 a.m. and I am still wanting that drink . . . I pencil his name in my diary for the following week—8.30 a.m. precisely—and know it will be changed by the afternoon . . .

S ENIOR THUG MAX CAVANAGH COMES INTO ANNE STEVENS' life at roughly the same time as her old friend Frances Smith. Stories of the past spill into the present. Changed lives. Everyday crime is the theme and figuring out who killed who and why Max Cavanagh is falling apart are only a few of the detections being made.

Only Lawyers Dancing has enough stylistic manners to be well behaved as a crime novel and enough quirky shifts to surprise and transform our ideas of contemporary crime myths and realities.

Mudrooroo

LONG RECOGNISED AS THE FIRST ABORIGINAL NOVELIST, Mudrooroo is one of the most fascinating authors writing in Australia. Changing his style as often as he has changed his name, Mudrooroo has continually tested the boundaries of fiction and of Aboriginality over the past thirty years.

In this first critical study of Mudrooroo's writing, Adam Shoemaker (author of *Black Words, White Page* and co-editor of *Paperbark*) focuses upon the work of this revolutionary stylist, from *Wild Cat Falling* (1965) to his most recent work, *The Kwinkan* (1993). This lively and informed analysis is accompanied by a revealing interview with Mudrooroo and a comprehensive bibliography.